LOOK WHO'S TALKING!

The Alemany Press

Other titles of interest

CHRISTISON, M.A.
English Through Poetry

DENNIS, J., GRIFFIN, S., and WILLS, R.
English Through Drama

MACULAITIS, J.D. and SCHERAGA, M.
What to do Before the Books Arrive

OLSEN, J.E. W·B
Communication-Starters and Other Activities for the ESL Classroom

SORRELLS, S. and BLOHM, C.
A Step-by-Step Guide to Setting up a School-Within-a-School

LOOK WHO'S TALKING!

A guide to the development of
successful conversation groups
in intermediate and advanced
E.S.L. classrooms.

MARY ANN CHRISTISON and
SHARRON BASSANO

Photographs of students by
Herbert Kahn and Sandra Hajdu

Illustrations by permission from
Japanese Border Designs
Theodore Menten
Dover Publications, Inc., N.Y.

PERGAMON PRESS

OXFORD · NEW YORK · TORONTO
SYDNEY · PARIS · FRANKFURT

The Alemany Press
2501 Industrial Parkway West
Hayward, CA 94545
800 227-2375 (415) 887-7070

The Alemany Press

| USA | The Alemany Press
2501 Industrial Parkway West
Hayward, CA 94545 USA
800 227-2375 (415) 887-7070 |

The Pergamon Press

U.K.	Pergamon Press Ltd., Headington Hill Hall, Oxford OX3 OBW, England
U.S.A.	Pergamon Press Inc., Maxwell House, Fairview Park, Elmsford, New York 10523, U.S.A
CANADA	Pergamon Press Canada Ltd., Suite 104, 150 Consumers Rd., Willowdale, Ontario M2J 1P9, Canada
AUSTRALIA	Pergamon Press (Aust.) Pty., Ltd., PO Box 544, Potts Point, N.S.W. 2011, Australia
FRANCE	Pergamon Press SARL, 24 rue des Ecoles, 75240 Paris, Cedex 05, France
FEDERAL REPUBLIC OF GERMANY	Pergamon Press GmbH, 6242 Kronberg-Taunus, Hammerweg 6, Federal Republic of Germany

British Library Cataloging in Publication Data

Christison, Mary Ann
Look Who's Talking
(Language teaching methodology series)
1. English language — Spoken English
2. English language — Study and   Teaching — Foreign Students
I. Title
II. Bassano, Sharron
428.3   PE1128.A2

ISBN 0-08029-445-6   (U.K.)
ISBN 0-88084-004-8   (U.S.A.)

Printed in the USA

4 5 6 7 8 9 0 0 9 8 7 6

TO OUR STUDENTS, OUR TEACHERS

Notes & acknowledgements

This book offers a wide variety of stimulating, relevant, fun, and exciting conversation activities. Many of these activities are our own creations, the result of a combined 21 years of classroom experience. Other activities come to us from experience in general communication-skills classes, self-awareness groups, and psychotherapy practice. These activities have been adapted especially to fit the language learning focus. The experienced teacher will also recognize among these pages our own variations of several tried-and-true ESL standbys such as "Strip Story," "Person Search," "20 questions," "Interviews," "Brain Teasers," and "Problem Solving." We have tried to cite references wherever possible; however, some of these activities have become such an integral part of so many teachers' ESL "grab-bags" and have appeared in so many journals, workshops, and ESL conferences that we have found impossible the task of tracking down the "originators." It is not our intention here to claim all the ideas in this book as our own. We only hope to offer you an orderly frame-work within which to work, a new "strategy-context" that will render these activities fail-proof in their presentation. We wish you and your students the best of success and the maximum of fun as you get to know yourselves and each other in your conversation groups.

Mary White

Sharron Bassano

Table of Contents

Large Group 91

Resources Guide 111

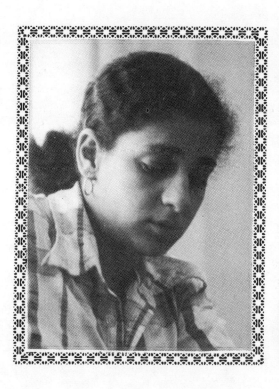 

Foreword

Traditional approaches to language teaching have usually required learners to perform in ways that are only indirectly related to actual language use, ways such as drills, memorization, short answers, answering questions about stories, and so on. Approaches utilizing such activities usually require the students to participate using someone else's meaning, meaning supplied by books or by teachers. Many hours are devoted to these types of learning activities partly because they are customary and partly because there are few really useful alternatives.

There are more immediate and meaningful ways to teach and learn languages, ways that make primary use of the learner's existing ability and desire to communicate and the meanings that they have to communicate. The difficulty with meaning-based teaching approaches till now has been that teachers accustomed to teaching language structure have not always known how to structure communication, especially for the purpose of teaching language.

Look Who's Talking gives teachers the tools to use in shaping classroom communication. It separates what has seemed right in language learning from what was customary but not really useful to students. By providing teachers with a large and useful set of classroom activities and the strategies with which to use them, the authors provide a way from the beginning to the end of language learning and give both students and teachers personal choices along the way.

The publication of this book is especially welcome as it is the first teacher-resource book which directly charts a path for meaning-based language learning.

Karl Krahnke, Ph.D.
June 1981

Introduction

Ask any student of English as a second language what it is that s/he wants most from the language class experience and nine times out of ten the answer will be, "more conversation practice." We have thought about this request frequently and have wondered just what our students mean. If students are living and studying in the United States, don't they have plenty of opportunity to practice their English? Isn't the free conversation waiting for them daily just out of the classroom door?

We believe that students are, in fact, asking for more of an opportunity to become themsevles in the new language. They want to become enthusiastically and authentically involved. They want to know that they are genuinely respected and treated as individuals by their teachers and classmates. It is so easy for our classes to become mechanistic and dull for the students. It is easier to provide rote drills and endless pattern practice for them than it is to devise meaningful and relevant communication. We may be giving them ample opportunities to manipulate their new language, but too little time to become truly involved.

Outside of class, our students may have the chance to interact with the clerk in the market, the postmaster or the bus driver, but personal communication is often only available with friends from the same native language background. Many times real conversation with native speakers of English is severely limited.

Being aware of the in-put students receive both in and out of the classroom, as teachers, we have often experimented with the free conversation session. Sometimes we succeed and we are able to touch our students in just the right spot and they "take off." Sometimes we see our great plans fall flat! It often seems like a case of good or back luck - no guarantees. Many times we put our students in a circle, give them a topic for discussion that we think is particularly stimulating and we see them just sit and look at one another in an embarrassing silence, constrained, nervous, tense. We end up bailing out the group and carrying the bulk of the dialog ourselves! Often, too, there is one agressive student who seems to feel a need to be the center of attention at all times, a student who shows little awareness of functional group interaction patterns, and even less self-discipline. Other times, we have one or two students who are either too shy to participate or who have such low self-esteem that they feel they have nothing of interest to offer the group. (What to I have to contribute? Who could possibly be interested in what I have to say?)

Another very real problem is that most of our foreign students come to us from an academic background that is typified by straight rows of desks, all eyes to the front on the teacher who is directing each classroom activity like a conductor leading an orchestra. They have had no experience in directing their own classroom use of language, and consequently fall apart when left to their own devices. Many subconsciously assume that learning is not possible without the teacher present.

We have come to believe that when conversation groups fail it is neither the fault of the activities presented, nor due to lack of creativity or energy expended on the part of the teacher. Hours are spent conscientiously developing and designing activities and topics to cue exciting and effective conversation among the students. Our hearts are in the right place! Rather, the problem lies with unrealistic expectations. We put a room full of strangers into a circle and we expect them to act as close friends before they even know or trust each other. We expect them to be well-versed in the dynamics of group process such as turn taking, interrupting, active listening, etc. We expect them to know how to deal with the more vocal members and draw out the more timid or self-conscious ones. They are expected to know how to conduct themselves as a cohesive entity with no previous experience at self-direction in the classroom. Too often we give them topics that are too hot to handle - topics that require a great deal of personal disclosure.

What we propose as a solution to these problems is a progressive format or **sequencing** of strategies in the conversation class which carefully prepares students, that systematically breaks down student stereotypes of classroom procedure and allows them to begin interacting democratically and independently. Through this approach, students learn step-by-step, functional interaction techniques at the same time the group spirit or trust is being built. By careful sequencing of strategies, plenty of attention can be given to the boisterous students in an acceptable manner and the quiet, retiring ones can be drawn into action in a painless procedure. All interpersonal activities should move from low-risk, non-personal content, such as games, information gathering, reporting, problem solving, etc., to activities which ask for the sharing of personal values, beliefs and feelings.

Through classroom experimentation, we have identified and worked with six activity categories or strategies.[†] They are: 1) restructuring, 2) one-centered, 3) unified group, 4) dyads, 5) small groups, and 6) large group. Each one of the hundred or so activities we introduce to our conversation classes fit into one of these strategies. The objectives and formats are as follows:

STRATEGY: Restructuring

OBJECTIVES:

1. To break down expected classroom structures.
2. To create opportunities for supportive behavior
3. To dispel fears and anxieties.
4. To relax both the student and the teacher.

Restructuring activities usually require the students to get up and out of their chairs and to interact physically as a group. There is minimal direction by the teacher. In fact, in most activities the teacher is full participant like any other student. Often the communication is done non-verbally, throuch action, drawings, or quickly written statements, and is usually non-personal.

[†] The six strategies were originally develped for a workshop entitled "A six-step approach to the conversation class" for TESOL '80 in San Francisco, presented by Mary Ann Christison, Karl J. Krahnke, and Thomas Schroeder.

STRATEGY: One-Centered

OBJECTIVES:
1. To provide each student with individual attention and acceptance from the entire group.
2. To increase the likelihood of contributions in the discussions which will follow later.

One-centered activities always put one student in the spotlight for a short time on a voluntary basis. Content can be either personal or non-personal, and, depending on a the student's self-confidence, may entail maximum or minimum verbalization, from the front of the class or in his or her seat.

STRATEGY: Unified Group

OBJECTIVES:
1. To develop cooperation among group members.
2. To emphasize each group member's value to the group.
3. To provide opportunities for group success.

Unified group activities require the participation of each group member. No one may bow out. Each person's contribution is essential to completion of the activity. The teacher is only minimally engaged in the activity, and content may be both personal or non-personal.

STRATEGY: Dyads

OBJECTIVES:
1. To get students accustomed to dealing openly with their own feelings, sensitivities, and emotions.
2. To provide opportunity for simple interaction with only one other class member at a time.
3. To develop sincere interpersonal communication in the second language.

STRATEGY: Small Group

OBJECTIVES:
1. To develop in each individual a growing sense of commitment to the group.
2. To develop trust and cooperation among group members.
3. To develop group interaction techniques that facilitate fair interaction.

Group activities require patience and good listening patterns. They require attention sharing, turn-taking, fair interruptions. The teacher is usually facilitator and participator.

STRATEGY: Large Group

OBJECTIVES: The objectives for large groups are the same as for small groups. The only difference is the inclusion of a wider range of individuals whom the student has learned to trust.

There are no hard and fast rules about the proper time to introduce new strategy types to your students. However, its seems to be a good idea to start with restructuring, unified group and one-centered activities, as these three types begin to change your students' attitudes about what learning entails, about their own self-image, and about the importance of cooperation in forming a positive class experience. When your group has reached the stage of being able to function in dyads and small groups, there will be occasions when you will want to return to earlier strategies for a time, just to reinforce these early learnings. For example, you may notice a certain disruptive competitive spirit forming. You may want to remind your group of the advantages of cooperation through a unified group activity or you may have a student who seems to be demanding too much personal attention to the detriment of the group. Plan a One Centered activity around him/her in order to provide that special needed attention! Do the same for a new student or one who seems to have withdrawn a little, to remind him/her of each individual's worth and importance to the group.

It has been our experience that students do benefit from conversation class activites, but free conversation can and must be structured. It requires careful sequencing of activities, careful preparation of the individuals involved and careful movement of topics from non-personal to self-disclosure content. With a gradual, methodical development of group interaction process and a building of group spirit over time, in conjunction with teacher imagination, creativity, and concern, you have the magic formula for fail-proof conversation groups.

Included in this book are 75 activities to illustrate how the objectives are met. As you read them, consider what additional activities you personally have done in your conversation classes which might fit into each category or strategy. The final section provides 75 additional sources which should provide you with even more ideas for your own activities, discussions, role-plays, games, etc.

We wish you success and satisfaction!

1. Restructuring

Every Body Votes

PROCEDURE:

Hang large newsprint sheets around the room, each sheet having as a heading a conversation topic - "Politics,", "Religion," "Family," "Fun and Recreation," "Work," "Love and Romance," "Friendship," etc. Ask students to consider what their personal favorite conversation area is, and to signify their choice by going over and standing by the chart. After all have noticed the balance of interests, ask them to move and go stand by the chart that is their least favorite topic of conversation. After all have gotten a feeling for who is in the class and what some of their interests might be, give them all colored pens and ask them to mill about the room considering each chart and ask them to write some "graffiti" - a comment, a statement or a question they might personally have regarding each topic. Let this activity continue until all have had a chance to write something and to read what others have written.

To process or complete this restructuring activity, you might ask the group as a whole how they felt doing this exercise, what they noticed, what they heard. Or they might sit down in small groups and comment on what they were compelled to write or on something they read that they didn't agree with.

Note: Every Body Votes may be organized around many different subjects. "Conversation Topics" is just one example. Try "Plans for a Saturday Night," "Vacation Spots," "Possessions — things we can't live without," "Household Chores," and "Classroom Activities." Use your imagination.

How Well Do You Know Me?

PROCEDURE:

Prepare a handout which lists 30 things which may be true about any given individual in the class — for example, **has brown hair, has been to Japan, likes chocolate ice cream,** etc. The handout should vary from class to class depending on the composition of the class. Make certain to include things the participants can observe about each other, i.e., **has brown hair** with things they cannot observe but have to ask of each other, i.e., **likes chocolate ice cream.** Move all the chairs out of the center of the room so that the class members can move about freely. Provide a handout for each individual in the group. A sample handout follows.

Instructions: You have just been given a handout which lists 30 things which may be true about any one person in this class. Your task is to find out which things are true about which person in this room. Some of the things which are true you will notice right away. For other things, you will have to ask the individual. If you find an individual who says that an item number is true, have the individual sign his/her name by the item. You will have ten minutes to get as many signatures as possible for **each** item. More than one signature on each item is possible. The winner is the person who can get the most signatures. You will have 10 minutes in which to get as many signatures as possible. The winner will receive a prize!

Variations on this activity have been presented many times at ESL conferences and conventions. Our thanks go to those who are probably the source of the idea behind these kinds of activities, Sidney Simon, Howie Kirschenbaum, and Leland Howe.
See resource guide in this book.

How Well Do You Know Me?

Instructions: Get as many signatures as possible for each number.

Rules: You must ask the question each time and your classmate must answer. It's against the rules to take the paper and start signing **your** name by everything which is true.

1. wears contacts_____

2. is married _____

3. is left-handed _____

4. wears glasses _____

5. is wearing a plaid shirt _____

_____

6. is not married _____

7. is a stranger to you _____

_____

8. has dimples _____

9. has the same color of eyes as you do

_____

10. is from your home country _____

_____

11. is wearing sandals _____

12. has a mustache _____

13. is from South America _____

_____

14. has another class with you_____

_____

15. dislikes American hamburgers

_____

16. has the same first initial as yours

_____

17. was born in the same month as you were

_____

18. has the same major as you do

_____

19. is from the Middle East _____

_____

20. has a watch on _____

21. is from Japan _____

22. is wearing black shoes _____

_____

23. has attended another school in the U.S.

_____

24. is your friend _____

25. has been in the U.S. longer than 5 months

_____

4

STRATEGY TYPE: Restructuring
PERSONAL ⊠ **NON-PERSONAL** ☐
TIME NEEDED: 20 minutes
MATERIALS: Colored paper (12x18) for each student, colored pens, pins

Introductions

PROCEDURE:

Give each student a piece of colored paper (12x18) and some colored pens. Ask them to do the following:

Make a picture of yourself that shows us how you feel today **or** a picture of yourself that shows us where you'd rather be, what you'd rather be doing or whom you'd rather be **with.** Under the picture, write three words that end with **-ing** that tell us three things you do very well. Over the picture write your first name.

Allow five or six minutes for this activity, then have the students pin the drawing to the front of their shirts and have them mill about **silently** for a few minutes. Ask them to get acquainted, to learn a little bit about each other only with their eyes. After they have done this, ask them to stop where they are and think about:

> Did you see anything similar to your drawing?
> Did you see something very different from your drawing?
> What did you see that interested you?
> Whom do you think you would like to talk with?
> Was there anything you didn't understand?

Now, ask them to mill about again, this time asking questions or making comments or pointing out similarities or differences. After this activity, you might want to ask each student to choose a partner, sit down, and find out more about that person.

Variations on this activity have been presented many times at ESL conferences and conventions. Our thanks go to those who are probably the source of the idea behind these kinds of activities, Sidney Simon, Howie Kirschenbaum, and Leland Howe.
See resource guide in this book.

STRATEGY TYPE: Restructuring
PERSONAL ☐ **NON-PERSONAL** ☒
TIME NEEDED: 15 minutes
MATERIALS: Miscellaneous pictures torn from magazines

Question Mill

PROCEDURE:

Pin a picture to each class member's back. Don't let the students see their own pictures. Have the students mill around the class asking questions about their pictures. e.g., **Am I a machine? Am I an animal?** or **Am I something to eat?,** until they discover what they "are." Instruct students that they may only answer **yes** or **no** to a question and that they may only ask yes/no questions. After ten minutes of asking and answering, find out who knows and who doesn't know "who they are."

This is a variation on the old parlor game "Twenty Questions."

What Are You Wearing?

PROCEDURE:

Give each student a strip of paper. Have them write a brief description of one thing they are wearing. Tell them to describe it carefully and clearly. It must be something they are wearing which can be seen.

Example: I am wearing a gold ring on the small finger of my left hand.

                    or

        I am wearing a red turtle-neck sweater.

Put all the slips of paper in a sack. Mix the pieces thoroughly. Have each student draw a slip from the sack. Make certain they draw someone else's slip. When all members of the group have a slip, give them the handout questions. Ask them to find the person described on the slip of paper and find out the answers to the questions.

Handout questions:
1. What's your name?
2. Where are you from?
3. What are you going to major in?
4. How long have you been in the U.S.?
5. How old are you?

Now give them small slips of paper again. This time they should write what their classmate is wearing. Follow the same procedure as before. Mix the papers, have the students draw from the sack, find the classmate described and ask the questions.

Follow-up:

Now have the students return to a large group. Stand by a student and ask one of the questions, i.e., **What's her name?** One of the people who has interviewed her will be able to supply the information. Continue this way until all class members have been involved.

Line Ups

PROCEDURE:

Ask your students to line up in the room according to a certain pattern (listed examples below). In order to form their lines, it will be necessary for them to speak with each other to determine their relative positions.

Use these ideas and invent your own!

1. Alphabetical order according to last names.

2. Alphabetical order according to native country name.

3. How long have you been in the United States?

4. How long have you studied English?

5. How many brothers and sisters do you have?

6. What time did you get up this morning?

7. What time did you go to bed last night?

8. How old are you?

9. How tall are you?

10. How many different girlfriends/boyfriends have you had?

11. How long is your hair?

12. Who is wearing the brightest color clothing?

13. How much money do you have in your pocket right now?

STRATEGY TYPE: Restructuring
PERSONAL ☐ **NON-PERSONAL** ☒
TIME NEEDED: 10 minutes
MATERIALS: Questions and answers for each student

Where's My Answer?

PROCEDURE:

Make a list of questions and answers similar to those given in the example exercise which follows. Each question or answer should be written on a separate sheet of paper. Put all the questions and answers in a small box or bag. Mix them thoroughly. Have each student take one slip of paper from the box. The number of questions and answers should be equal to the number of students in the class.

Instructions:

I will now pass a box around. You will each take a slip of paper. Don't look at it until you are told to do so (repeat). On the slip of paper you will find a question or an answer. If you have a question, try to find the person who has your answer. If you have an answer, try to find the person who has the question for your answer. As soon as you have found your question or answer, stand by that person. You will have 3 minutes to find your partner.

Sample questions:

Q 1. How many sides does a triangle have?
A 1. A triangle has three sides.
Q 2. Who is President of the U.S.?
A 2. (Ronald Reagan) is President of the U.S.?
Q 3. How many states are there in the U.S.?
A 3. There are 50 states in the U.S.
Q 4. Does the sun rise in the east or west?
A 4. The sun rises in the east.

Q 5. In what month is Christmas celebrated?
A 5. Christmas is celebrated in December.
Q 6. How many days are in our U.S. calendar year?
A 6. There are 365 days in a year.
Q 7. In what state is (Los Angeles)?
A 7. Los Angeles is in California.

Make as many questions as you need for your class.

Note: Notice these questions could be answered by almost anyone. Teachers should feel free to adapt the questions to suit the needs of their class.

Follow-up activities:

Have the students say the questions and answers individually to make certain the group agrees with the answer. Prepare two sets of questions. Use the activity again.

Add Your Own!

2. One-centered

STRATEGY TYPE: One Centered
PERSONAL ☒ **NON-PERSONAL** ☐
TIME NEEDED: 15 minutes
MATERIALS: Questions handouts

On Focus

PROCEDURE:

Thought Gathering: Give each student a copy of a list of possible interview questions and allow them a few minutes of quiet reflection — a chance to think about how they might answer the questions (Interview question examples on following page).

Sharing: Ask a volunteer to come up to the front of the class and sit comfortably in a chair. Allow group members to ask questions from the list or their own original questions to the volunteer. The one being interviewed has the right to say "I pass" on any question that he or she can't or doesn't want to answer. She/he also has the opportunity after eight minutes of interviewing to ask back to members of the group any question that was posed to him/her. Be sure that the group understands that there is a time limit, a right to pass, and an opportunity to ask the three questions back. (Probably it is best to do no more than two interviews at any one class session.)

A VARIATION OF ON FOCUS FOR SMALL GROUPS

Sharing: Have students form groups of four. One student in each group will be on focus for five minutes. The other three members will take turns asking the focus person questions either from the list or original ones. The focus person has the right to pass on any question that she/he can't or doesn't choose to answer, and will also have the opportunity to ask a question **back** to any group member when the focus is finished. Ask them to be aware of their listening patterns — to notice when they want to interrupt or suggest answers to their own questions or take the focus back to themselves. Ask them to concentrate on truly listening. Each student in the group will have a turn at being on focus. You might want to have a little bell or some other way to signal the change of focus so that the turn will be passed around the circle and all groups will more or less stay together and finish about the same time.

Variations on this activity have been presented many times at ESL conferences and conventions. Our thanks go to those who are probably the source of the idea behind these kinds of activities, Sidney Simon, Howie Kirschenbaum, and Leland Howe.
See resource guide in this book.

Interview Questions for ON FOCUS

1. What is something you really want to learn to do before you die?
2. Where do you think you will be five years from now? Doing what?
3. How would your life be changed if there were no T.V.?
4. Tell me about someone special in your family.
5. Are you anxious to get married? Why? Why not?
6. What kind of social evenings do you like?
7. What is a current problem that you have?
8. Who is someone that you are always happy to see? Why?
9. If you found $50 in the street, what would you do with it?
10. How do you spend your weekends?
11. Where do you go when you want to be alone?
12. Do you enjoy sports? Which ones?
13. Whom do you miss the most in your country?
14. What is the worst work you have ever done for money?

1. Would you consider marrying someone who was not of your race or cultural background?
2. What is something really scary that happened to you?
3. What is your favorite food?
4. How do you feel about homosexuality?
5. What is something you have that you would hate to lose?
6. What kind of advice did your mother give you when you were young?
7. Who is the "boss" in your family? How do you know?
8. What is a present you would like to receive?
9. Who helps you in the United States? Do you have a special American friend?
10. Did your parents take you to any sort of religious services when you were a child? Will you take your children to learn religious teachings?
11. What are you saving money for?
12. Who gave you your first romantic kiss?
13. Do you believe in life after death?
14. Do you smoke? How do you feel about laws that control smoking in public areas?

What Am I?

PROCEDURE:

Prepare 20 three by five cards with the name of an animal or a thing written on each one. These items can range from easy ones like **tree, cat, dog, elephant,** and **book** to more complicated ones like **glue, coca-cola,** and **matches.**

Instructions: Ask for a volunteer from the class. Have the student come forward and turn around with his/her back to the rest of the class. Now show the class one of the three by five cards with the name of an animal or thing written on it. Pin the card on the student's back. The student now becomes that thing or animal, i.e. **dog, cat, soap,** etc. The volunteer student does not know what he/she is, but the class does. The only way for the volunteer student to find out what he/she is, is to ask the class questions. Class members give only the information asked for. Each volunteer is allowed to ask 10 questions of 10 different class members. After five questions, the student may ask one of the class members for a **hint.** If the student does not get the correct answer after 10 questions, the class may give him/her hints until he/she finds the answer. Make certain all class members understand the rules before the activity begins.

Note to the teacher: Do two or three a session, not the whole class in one day.

Instructions: For the shy, less verbal student, turn the activity around. Let the spotlighted person know what the card says but not the rest of the class. The class members must ask the question to find out what's on the card; the focused person only has to answer "yes" or "no." This is obviously a very painless, low-risk way to be the star of the show.

16

STRATEGY TYPE: One Centered
PERSONAL ☐ NON-PERSONAL ☒
TIME NEEDED: 15 minutes
MATERIALS: none

Experiences

PROCEDURE:

Thought Gathering: Ask your students to complete the following sentences.

> A good thing which happened to me today was . . . .
> and
> A bad thing which happened to me today was . . . .

Give them three minutes to think about the sentences and complete them. You could also have them write their responses in the form of a letter to you.

Sharing: Divide the class into small groups. Each person within the group should have a chance to share his/her experiences while the others listen. Give them two minutes apiece. Let them know when the two minutes are up.

Follow-up: Have them return to a large group. Share experiences. Find out how they felt during their experiences. Let students volunteer. Give plenty of time.

STRATEGY TYPE: One Centered
PERSONAL ☒ **NON-PERSONAL** ☐
TIME NEEDED: 30 minutes
MATERIALS: none

Teachers

PROCEDURE:

Initiate a discussion based on the idea that "everyone is a teacher," that "anything we can do well, we can teach someone else." Ask your students about teachers they have had, not just in school environments, but in their whole life — perhaps, friends or relatives who have spent time with them helping them learn various skills. Give them a few minutes to gather ideas about what skills they have, what skills they could teach to someone else. (Most likely you will get a lot of "humble noises," a lot of protests about not knowing how to do anything special that anyone would be interested in learning. Remind them that, indeed, they do! For example, many of your students could be "teachers" of their native language, native cooking, origami, soccer, swimming, yoyo, knot-tying, make-up or hair styling, dance, horse-back-riding, etc. Give them a few ideas to get them started.)

After a few minutes, put each student on focus for a few seconds, asking them to share with the class some things they could teach the others. Have them tell you who taught them. Make a list on the board of all their collective skills and they will be amazed at the diversity of knowledge that they have each brought to class with them. Propose a special week of demonstrations by students.

As a follow-up, you might want to have them write a short essay on "My Best Teacher," emphasizing that this doesn't necessarily mean a school teacher.

I Am

PROCEDURE:

Thought Gathering: Ask each student to number from 1 to 10 on a piece of paper and finish the sentence, "I am. . . ." ten times. Most answers will be somewhat outer directed, i.e., I am Juan's wife. I am a cannery worker, I am Luisa, I am a student. It is better not to model any sort of answer or give examples. See what they come up with.

Sharing: Ask for a volunteer to come up in front of the class, leaving his/her paper behind, allow various students to pose the questions: Who are you? And who else are you? Are you anyone else? You might want to ask a couple of volunteers to come up so that they can see the diversity (or similarity) of the answers. Another idea is to ask your volunteers to tell you which "role" they like best, which is most important right now, which role they wish they didn't have.

Variations: This activity can well be expanded into a writing exercise or a small group activity, sharing their feelings about all the different people they are, depending on who they are with. You might also point out that many of the things they listed were pertaining to other people — outer sorts of "I am's. . ." You could then ask them to make a private list of who they are **inside** — identities that perhaps they keep hidden. Some of your students might be interested in doing this as a writing assignment.

Variations on this activity have been presented many times at ESL conferences and conventions. Our thanks go to those who are probably the source of the idea behind these kinds of activities, Sidney Simon, Howie Kirschenbaum, and Leland Howe.
See resource guide in this book.

STRATEGY TYPE: One Centered
PERSONAL ☐ **NON-PERSONAL** ☒
TIME NEEDED: 25 minutes
MATERIALS: "catch-all" bag, household items, handout

The "Catch-All" Bag

PROCEDURE:

Preparation: Bring a "catch-all" bag to class containing a variety of small items found around the house, e.g., **clothespins, strainers, napkin holders, toothbrushes, lids, can openers,** etc. Place all the items on a large table. Give each item a number. Prepare a list of the items on a handout.

Instructions: Give each student a list of items. Have them try to match the item on the list with the numbered object on the table. They should write the number beside each item on the list. Allow about 10 minutes for them to match all the items in the list to the objects. Encourage them to talk and discuss during the activity. After 10 minutes, go over the identification of the items in a large group. Students will then know if they have the correct answers.

Groups: Divide the class into small groups. Give each group an equal number of objects. For example, with 20 items and 4 groups, each group would get five items. The group should pick one person to go first. That person will try to name the objects correctly and give the number. If she/he makes a mistake in identifying the object, the other members should raise their hands but not say anything. Each person takes a turn. Then all groups switch objects so they have a chance to work with all the items on the list.

Follow-up: Have the students return to the large group. Find out what each item is used for.

Add Your Own!

3. Unified group

Floor Map

PROCEDURE:

Tell students to imagine that the floor of the classroom is a map of the world. Point out to them where Europe, China, and South America are so that they will have an idea of their direction. Ask them to go and stand in their native country. They will have to speak with each other quite a lot in order to determine their relative positions. (If all of your students are from one country, have the floor be a map only of that country and ask them to stand in their city or province.)

Give them a question to consider for a few minutes while they are standing in their country or city. The question will be about that particular place. Give them a minute to gather thoughts, then ask three or four of them to share their ideas with the others (still standing in place). Examples of question might be:

> What is something special that you remember about that place,
>
> some special feeling or scene?
> What are the circumstances that caused you to leave there?
>
> Who is someone you think about a lot who lives in that place?
>
> What is something you didn't like about your country?
>
> What is the most beautiful thing you have ever seen in your country?

After they have shared the first question, ask them to consider another and get three or four different students to respond. Continue until you have worked with four or five questions.

Variation: Imagine the room to be a map of the city in which you now live. What do you find especially valuable about the place where you now live? Who is someone in your neighborhood who helps you? Listens to you? What is a special place in your neighborhood that you visit often? What is a problem you sometimes have in your neighborhood. Are there many people from other countries living in your neighborhood? Is there one special ethnic group there?

Variation: After unified group sharing, the class may be divided into small groups for most personal or expanded sharing of the questions you have posed.

Variations on this activity have been presented many times at ESL conferences and conventions. Our thanks go to those who are probably the source of the idea behind these kinds of activities, Sidney Simon, Howie Kirschenbaum, and Leland Howe.
See resource guide in this book.

STRATEGY TYPE: Unified Group
PERSONAL ☐ **NON-PERSONAL** ☒
TIME NEEDED: 30 minutes
MATERIALS: 3"x5" index cards, cut lengthwise

Proverbs

PROCEDURE:

Part One

Ask your students to prepare a list of three or four proverbs or sayings from their native country. You may have to help them with the translation. Give them some examples of ones from our culture, e.g.:

> A stitch in time saves nine.
> Don't cry over spilled milk.
> You can lead a horse to water, but you can't make him drink.
> A bird in the hand is worth two in the bush.

When you have helped them put the proverbs in order, have them copy them on small cards which have been torn in half, writing half of the saying on one piece and half of it on the other. Ask them to print or write as clearly as possible. (If there is a handwriting problem, you might want to take their ideas home with you and type them up yourself.) Ask your students not to share their contributions with the group yet.

Part Two

Take all the pieces, shuffle them and pass them out evenly among the students. Tell them they have to mill around reading each others' cards until they find the other half of their sayings. When a pair has been found, have them put them down on their desks. When all pieces are reunited, ask the students to read them out loud and try to figure out what the moral or message is really saying.

STRATEGY TYPE: Unified Group
PERSONAL ☐ **NON-PERSONAL** ☒
TIME NEEDED: 25 minutes
MATERIALS: One puzzle for each person or each group

Puzzle It Out

PROCEDURE:

Instructions to the Participants:

1. Your group has been given enough puzzle pieces to form six separate puzzles.
2. Each puzzle is made up of three or four pieces and when put together forms an 8" by 10" rectangle.
3. There are two different colored puzzles in each set, for example, orange puzzles and white puzzles. Each puzzle is only one color. You may not mix colors in your own puzzle.

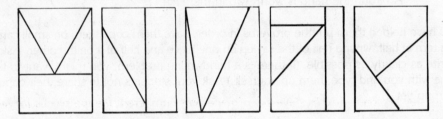

4. Please put all of the pieces together on the table (or floor) in front of your group. Mix them up very well, spread them out and be sure that no number or letter is visible on the puzzle pieces (the numbers and letters are on the **back** side of each piece and your puzzle will not match if numbers or letters are showing!)
5. Everyone in the group takes three or four puzzle pieces at random to begin the activity.
6. The object of the activity is for each member of the group to form his/her own puzzle and only when each member of the group has a rectangle that is 8" by 10" is the activity finished.

7. **Rules**

    A. You may **not speak** to any other member about puzzle pieces.
    B. You may **not take** any pieces from someone else.
    C. Pieces you need, however, may be **given** to you. Your group members must notice what piece you need and give it to you willingly, to help you form your puzzle.
    D. Please do not ask for or overtly signal for what you want!

8. Try the activity again. This time you may take anything you need, but still no talking.

Instructions for making puzzles:

Take five sheets of orange paper and cutting them all at one time on the paper cutter, make puzzles something like this: or this:

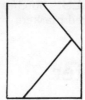 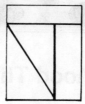

Being careful to not mix the pieces, number the pieces of each orange puzzle, then separate them into little stacks with a clip, thus:

  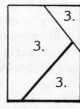 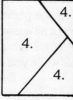 

Follow the same procedure in five or six different colors, each color being a slightly different pattern.

When all of your colored puzzles have been made and numbered, file the pieces for six puzzles together in one manila folder, three orange and three blue in one folder, three green and three yellow in another, etc. (Each folder will then be ready to use by a group of six students.)

Follow-up questions:

1. How did you feel about the lack of verbal communication?
2. How did you communicate with the other group members?
3. When we couldn't talk, I felt _____.
4. When we were taking, I noticed _____.
5. When we were giving, it was _____.

STRATEGY TYPE: Unified Group
PERSONAL ☒ **NON-PERSONAL** ☐
TIME NEEDED: 30 minutes
MATERIALS: butcher paper, colored paper, colored markers

Mood Thermometer

PROCEDURE:

Introduce this activity by holding up sheets of paper of various colors. Initiate a discussion of "What color is happy?" "What color is angry?" "What color do you think of when you feel jealous?" Continue presenting feelings and emotions in conjunction with a color symbol. Let them tell you. There is no right answer. Green might be one person's "envy" another person's "sick" and still another person's "insecure." That's okay. Accept all answers, and expect many varied reports! Then, ask them, "What color are you feeling today? Why? What is happening in your life that causes you to feel that color?" Let them just think about this while you draw the following thermometer on a long piece of newsprint or butcher paper.

Explain to the students that you would like them to come up one at a time and choose a color marker that is the color they are feeling today. Ask them to write their first name on the thermometer, high or low or in the middle, depending on how "high" they are feeling.

When all students have come up and written their names, it should be very evident who is feeling really good and who is having a terrible day. Have them observe how graphic this is and how very often we are not really aware of others' feelings unless we ask or unless they make a point to tell us.

You might want to complete this exercise by having students form smaller groups and do some sentence finishing around the circle as follows:

> I usually feel really happy when I . . .
> The thing that makes me the angriest is . . .
> The last time I cried was . . . because . . .
> Sometimes I am impatient when . . .
> The most frustrating thing I can think of is . . .

STRATEGY TYPE: Unified Group
PERSONAL ☐ **NON-PERSONAL** ☒
TIME NEEDED: 30 minutes
MATERIALS: One cartoon strip
for each group

Shadow Acting

PROCEDURE:

Prepare a three-frame cartoon-type strip with all the figures in shadows. Ink out the figures so that the situation and emotions are not readily apparent. (There are no facial expressions to go by. See example on the following page.) Divide students into groups equal to the number of different figures in the strip. Give **one** copy of the strip to each group.

Instructions

You have each been given a three-frame strip of shadow figures. Your responsibility is to decide what is going on in your strip. Each person should be one of the shadow figures. Write a dialogue or conversation for your strip. Be prepared to act it out. Each group will be given 20 minute. Talk and decide what you want to do. Have fun!

When all groups are finished creating their dialogues, invite volunteer groups to come act it out in front of the class

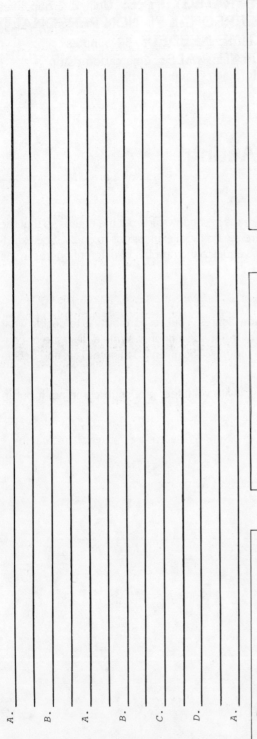

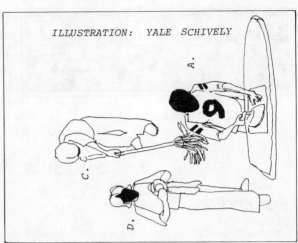

ILLUSTRATION: YALE SCHIVELY

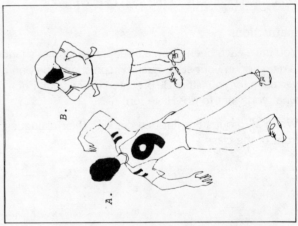

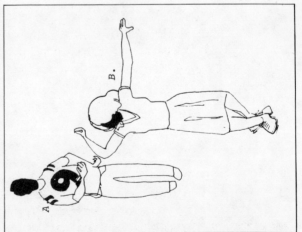

STRATEGY TYPE: Unified Group
PERSONAL ☐ **NON-PERSONAL** ☒
TIME NEEDED: 30 minutes
MATERIALS: Handout questions

Mystery Guests

PROCEDURE:

1. Invite a guest to your class. It can be someone from the community or school, preferably someone your students do not know or have not seen.

2. Give each student a copy of the "mystery guest questions." The class will have ten minutes to find as must about the mystery guest as possible. Each question should be asked only once. All the students should take notes for all questions on their individual papers. Questions which are not asked should also be noted. After 10-15 minutes, thank the mystery guest and invite him/her to come back for the last five minutes of class.

3. Divide the students into groups of five to eight. Each group will be a team. The teams will be asked questions about the mystery guest. All team members must participate. If a member answers the questions correctly, the team gets a point. If the question is answered incorrectly, the team misses the point. A group member does not have to answer alone. If s/he **asks** for help, the group can help. If a question is asked which the mystery guest did not answer, the person answering the questions should say so. This also receives a point.

4. Stop when each group has had a chance to have each person participate.

5. Total points. Give a small prize to the winning team.

6. Invite the mystery guest back for 5 minutes of additional questions and informal discussion.

Mystery Guest Questions

When is your birthday? What does your name mean?
What are your favorite things to do?
What is your favorite season?
What is the funniest thing you have ever done?
Have you ever won a contest? Where? How?
What countries have you visited?
What are you studying and why?
What kind of person would you like to become?
What sports do you like or participate in?
Who is one of your favorite people?
What is your favorite holiday? Why?
What is your favorite age to be?
Do you have any pets?
Who were you named after? Why?
When were you the most scared in your life?
Why did you come to the U.S.A.?
Do you want to live in the city (a big one) or a small town?
What instruments do you play?

STRATEGY TYPE: Unified Group
PERSONAL □ **NON-PERSONAL** ☒
TIME NEEDED: 20 minutes
MATERIALS: none

Lonely Hearts

PROCEDURE:

For this exercise, your students must already be well acquainted. Have each student write his/her name on a small piece of paper and put the piece of paper in a "hat." Each student then draws a name secretly from the hat. (If a student draws his/her own name, it is okay.) Tell the students that they are going to help find a wife or a husband for the student whose name is on their slip of paper. The way in which they will do this is by writing an ad for the lonely hearts or relationships (or introductions) column for the newspaper. Ask them to write in the first person, and describe their classmate physically, describe his/her personality and interests and personal data. If they are not sure, they can guess.

An example might begin: I am a man, 26 years old. I am tall and very thin. I don't have much money, but I am looking for work. I am always happy and I love popular music, beer and movies . . . . . etc.

After your students have written (and ask them to write as clearly as possible!) their "ads," collect them and post them on the walls around the clasroom. Let them do a "gallery walk" milling about the room reading the descriptions and if they think they know who is being described on the paper, have them write their guess. After a few minutes, find out if their guesses were correct. Then check with the student who was written about to see if the description is accurate to their satisfaction!

Ideas for 'strip stories' are shared at every conference and convention of ESL. We believe the original source to be Robert E. Gibson, "The Strip Story: A Catalyst for Communication", TESOL QUARTERLY, June 1975. See also, Alice Blows a Fuse in our resource guide.

STRATEGY TYPE: Unified Group
PERSONAL □ NON-PERSONAL ⊠
TIME NEEDED: 40 minutes
MATERIALS: A story part for each
student

Getting It All Together

PROCEDURE:

Find a short story or make up a story with a very simple plot. Divide the story into parts equal to the number of students in the class. Type each part on a separate piece of paper. Give each student a part of the story in random order. The task is for the class to put the story back together again. Students will have to understand what is contained in each part and will have to ask each other questions in order to discover where the part they have fits into the main plot of the story.

Instructions: You have just been given a slip of paper with a sentence on it. This sentence is part of a larger story. Each member of your group has one sentence from the story. You will now have 5 minutes to memorize the sentence on your paper. After you have memorized your sentence, give the paper to me.

Now give the students 20 minutes to put the story back together again from memory. After the students feel they have the correct order, have them tell the story to the rest of the class. Each individual in the group must remember his/her portion of the story in order for it to be successful.

Here are two sample stores:

Story #1 (Intermediate)
A very unusual thing happened to Bill last Friday. Although he usually works until 5:00 o'clock, he stayed until 6:00 on Friday and caught the last bus home. On the bus he sat by a very unusual woman. She didn't look unusual; she just acted unusual. During their conversation she abruptly stood up and yelled. Bill was embarrassed and so was the woman. She apologized again and again, claiming she didn't know what had happened. Bill had almost forgotten about the incident until he saw the same woman today. She noticed Bill and ran to catch him. She explained that she had been hypnotized at a lecture on Friday. Everytime someone said the word **wonderful,** she stood up and yelled. Bill had apparently used the word during the conversation on the bus. The hypnotist had forgotten to do something. She said she was fine now. Bill and the woman laughed and laughed. They agreed to see each other again soon.

Story #2 (Beginning)
Mary and Jane usually ride to school with a friend. Yesterday, they rode the bus. Their friend was sick. The bus took them on a different route. First, it stopped at the park. Mary loved all the flowers. She wanted to stay and enjoy them. Next, it stopped at the market. Jane loves markets. She wanted to stay and shop. There wasn't time. Both women stayed on the bus. They really enjoyed their ride. Now they are going to take the bus everyday.

35

Crosswork Groups

PROCEDURE:

Divide the class into groups of three to five. Give the groups the crosswork handout below.

Each group will have five minutes to get as many different words on their crosswork patterns as possible. Before anyone can go twice, everyone must go once. Points are given equal to the number of letters in the words. Group members must be patient. Participation from each member is of primary importance. Look at the examples below:

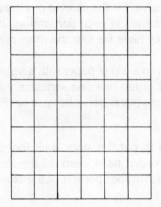

This group was able to make four words. They receive the following points:

Students	=	8
Tooth	=	5
House	=	5
Soap	=	4
Total		22 points

Making the words together requires the attention and help of every individual in the group. It is sometimes hard because different people see different things.

Add Your Own!

4. Dyads

STRATEGY TYPE: Dyads
PERSONAL ☐ **NON-PERSONAL** ☒
TIME NEEDED: 20 minutes
MATERIALS: A cartoon strip for each group

Cartoon Strip

PROCEDURE:

Form groups of four. Give each group one Xerox of a three or four frame cartoon strip from the Sunday paper, from which all the dialogue has been removed. Ask them as a group to consider the picture sequence carefully and to write what they think the characters are saying. Ask them to discuss it first, deciding on all the possibilities, then have them appoint a "secretary" to write in what they agree upon. Have them act it out if they want to.

When it looks as if each group is finished (possibly 15 minutes?), have them report to the larger group what they created. (See example next page.)

We are not sure of the original source of using cartoons, but we have found some references:
Audio-Visual Aids For Teaching English, Salah A. El-Araby, 1974, Longman, Inc.
Visual Materials for the Language Teacher, Andrew Wright, 1976, Longman Inc.

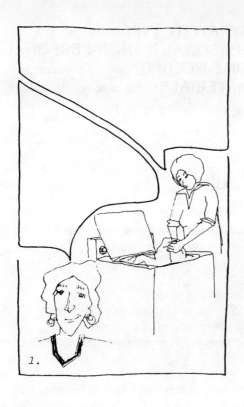

1.

2.

3.

4.

This Week

PROCEDURE:

Thought gathering: Have students make a quadrant labeled **This Week.** Ask them to consider answers to the following questions and write them briefly, one in each square:

What is a decision that you made this week?
What is something you did to make someone happy this week?
What is a small (or great!) success you had this week?
What is one compliment you received from someone this week?

Sharing: Choose a partner from the other side of the room, sit down with him or her and share two things from your week. Students may change partners and tell about their week several times. It is good repetition practice for them and the listener is still interested. This also gives them a chance to experience different accents, levels of proficiency and reactions from their various classmates.

Variations on this activity have been presented many
times at ESL conferences and conventions. Our thanks
go to those who are probably the source of the idea
behind these kinds of activities, Sidney Simon, Howie
Kirschenbaum, and Leland Howe.
See resource guide in this book.

STRATEGY TYPE: Dyads
PERSONAL ☐ NON-PERSONAL ☒
TIME NEEDED: 20 minutes
MATERIALS: 8"x10" newsprint
prepared cards or dittos

Where Do I Put It?

PROCEDURE:

The following four activities involve one student giving directions to his or her partner. A screen of some sort is set up between the two students who sit facing each other so that they can see each other's face and hear each other clearly but can **not** see each other's paper or materials. A manila file folder opened out and set on edge works fine for a screen or barrier.

Activity #1

One student has a blank sheet which he or she folds into nine squares and then opens out to use as a game board. The partner has a dittoed sheet that has nine squares with a small simple illustration in each square. The illustrations might be something like a cup and saucer, a cat, a tennis racket, an old car, a woman's shoe, a garbage can, a flag, a brush and a flower. The student with the illustrated sheet must tell his partner what to draw and where to draw it with as much detail as possible. He or she may not use his or her hands and may not show the drawings to the partner. When they are finished they should compare papers. You might have them then switch roles, using another prepared ditto with different illustrations.

Activity #2

Give all student a piece of paper and have them fold it into nine squares and open it out to form a game board. Give both of the partners an identical set of nine picture cards. Tell the students they must place the pictures on the game board in exactly the same positions, but they must not look at each other's board or pieces. Have one student decide to be the speaker, the other, the listener. The speaker describes the pictures and tells the listener where to place them. When all the pieces are in place, have them compare and then switch roles.

45

Activity #3

Give all students a piece of blank paper and have them fold it into nine squares. Have them open it out to use as a game board. Give both students a set of nine "shapes" that are cut out of tag board. (Each set of shapes is identical; a set is represented below. It obviously takes some time to prepare these sets, but it's well worth the effort and they can be used over and over!) The activity is conducted exactly as **Activity #2,** except that it is more difficult in that the pieces are hard to describe. You might want them to be sure and know the phrase, "It looks a little bit like a . . . ."

Activity #4

Give each student a piece of blank paper. Give one person in each pair a list of nouns. The person with the list must instruct the other person what to draw and where to draw it. They **both** must draw the picture on their papers and then compare when finished. Any verbal cues are okay - one simple word or a long lengthy description, but no hand language or showing! Some words for the list might be hammer, comb, snake, spoon, lamp, ship, sheep, map, or mop. (Other minimal pairs make good practice if you can find some that are easy to draw!)

Blind Faith

PROCEDURE:

Divide the class into groups of two. Explain the blindfold and demonstrate how to use it so that when it is in place the individual wearing it cannot see. Give each student a set of "leading instructions" (see examples below).

Instructions: You have each been given a set of instructions. Read the instructions carefully and make certain you understand exactly what to do. Do not show the instructions to your partner. If your instructions are marked #1, you will begin. Blindfold your partner. Make certain she/he cannot see. Then, lead your partner through the course in the instructions. **Be very careful.** Your partner cannot see and must rely on you to lead the way safely. Hold hands or lock arms. Your partner has to trust you!

Sample #1
Take your partner out of the classroom door. Turn right. Go up the stairs to the second floor. Turn your partner around in a circle five or six times. Follow the upstairs hall west. Return to the first floor by the back stairs. Bring your partner back to the class.

Sample #2
Take your partner out of the classroom. Turn left just outside the door. Follow the hall south and turn right at the end. Stop. Turn your partner around five or six times. Go back along the same hall and return to the classroom.

Note: Leading instructions will have to be prepared according to the location of your own particular classroom.

PROCEDURE:

Divide students into dyads again. This time they should have a different partner. Give each individual the following set of questions. Have them find out as much as possible about their feelings during the activity. After five minutes ask them to change and return to their original partner.

Follow-up activity: After the students have completed work in the dyads, have the class return to the large group size. Encourage a question and answer type forum. Use the sample questions to stimulate discussion.

Questions:

1. Do you like to be in the dark? (Why or why not?)
2. How did you feel when your partner put on your blindfold?
3. How did you feel when your partner turned you around? Were you confused?
4. How did you feel toward your partner?
5. Was it hard to trust your partner?
6. Did you trust your partner?
7. If yes, was it hard to trust? If no, why not?
8. Was your partner careful?
9. Were you scared?
10. Did your partner do things to make you frightened?
11. Did you do things to frighten your partner?
12. Did your partner go too slow or too fast for you?
13. Did you get mixed up?
14. Was the blindfold placed so you couldn't see?
15. Did you talk during the exercise?
16. What things did you say?

Variations on this activity have been presented many times at ESL conferences and conventions. Our thanks go to those who are probably the source of the idea behind these kinds of activities, Sidney Simon, Howie Kirschenbaum, and Leland Howe.
See resource guide in this book.

Distance And Space

PROCEDURE:

1. Divide your students into pairs. Have them go to opposite sides of the classroom and face each other. Give them each a copy of the handout material and instruct them to ask the first three questions. They should write the answers.

2. When they have all had a chance to answer the questions, have everyone stop. Ask some of the questions. Call on different students to supply the answers. Have students ask the questions.

3. Find out how they feel being so far away from the person they are talking to. Give sufficient time for thought gathering.

4. Instruct them to step about four feet closer to their partner and ask the next three questions. When they have had a chance to answer have them stop. Find out how they feel. Give sufficient time for thought gathering. (Depending on the size of the classroom, the distance you ask them to move may vary.)

5. Now ask your students to start walking slowly toward their partners until they are only three inches away. Stop. Find out how they feel. Allow time for thought gathering. (Students do not have to remain in so close a position. This will be uncomfortable for most students. Have them experience the feeling and break away.)

6. Ask the students to back up until they are at a comfortable distance for carrying on a conversation.

7. Look around the room. Is everyone at the same distance from their partners?

8. The distance you feel comfortable from your partner is called your "personal space."

9. Do you think your personal space is the same with all people?

10. Do you stand close to people you know better?

11. Observe people in your everyday life. How close do Americans normally stand?

12. Is your partner standing closer than you are comfortable with? Is the opposite true? (These questions are for thought gathering only.)

Handout questions for distance:

1. What's your address?
2. Do you have a telephone? Why or why not?
3. What's your favorite thing to do in this class?
4. How many times have you moved since you've been in the United States?
5. Where do you usually shop for groceries?
6. How often do you usually shop?

Note to the teacher: These example questions will need to be adapted to fit the need of your particular language class.

STRATEGY TYPE: Dyads
PERSONAL ☐ **NON-PERSONAL** ☒
TIME NEEDED: 15 minutes
MATERIALS: Category questions for each student

Back To Back

PROCEDURE:

Arrange desks in the room so they are back-to-back with each other. Divide the students into two groups, category (A) and category (B). Category (A) students will face in one direction and category (B) students will face the other direction. Each student will have a specific set of questions to ask his/her partner. Students will have copies of **their** category question only. This requires careful listening. These questions are prepared by the teacher in advance. Allow space on the question sheet for students to make notes for answers. After the students have finished with the interviews (allow no more then 10 minutes), have them form a circle and discuss their answers and what feelings they had about being unable to face their partner. Focus on some of the obvious advantages of face-to-face communication (e.g., facial expression, gestures, etc.). Find out if they had to repeat a lot. Was it difficult for them to understand? Why was it difficult?

Have the students get with their partner again. This time they will use face-to-face positions for the interviews. Provide them with a new set of questions. Allow times for discussion after this segment.

Note to the teacher: Example questions follow. You will want to adapt them to fit the particular needs of your class.

Set I
Category A Questions
for Back-to-back communication

1. Where were you born?
2. What is your native language?
3. Do you have any brothers or sisters?
4. How long have you been in the United States?
5. What is your favorite food?
6. What is your favorite color?
7. What is your favorite television show?
8. Why is it your favorite show?
9. Do you smoke?
10. Are you married?

50

Set II
Category A Questions
for Face-to-face communication

1. Can you drive a car?
2. What is your favorite sport?
3. What is the biggest problem you're having in learning English?
4. Name something important you have noticed about American people, something you have observed.
5. Do you like to get up early in the morning or would you rather sleep in?

Set I
Category B Questions
for Back-to-back communication

1. How long have you been in the United States?
2. What is the biggest problem you're having in learning English?
3. What is your favorite television show?
4. Why is it your favorite show?
   (Why don't you have a favorite show?)
5. Do you like to get up early in the morning or would you rather sleep in?
6. Do you smoke?
7. Does it bother you if people smoke in rooms when there is no way for the smoke to escape?
8. What is your favorite food?
9. What is your favorite color?
10. Do you wear your favorite color very often?
    Why or why not?

Set II
Category B Questions
for Face-to-face communication

1. How many brothers and sisters do you have?
2. Where do you live?
3. Where were you born?
4. Do you like eating in fast food restaurants like Dees and McDonalds?
5. What country would you like to visit which you haven't visited yet?

STRATEGY TYPE: Dyads
PERSONAL ☐ **NON-PERSONAL** ☒
TIME NEEDED: 25 minutes
MATERIALS: none

Word Association

PROCEDURE:

Tell your students that you are going to call out a list of words one at time and that you would like them to write that word and then write down the first word that comes to their mind after they have written your word. (They may also write a short phrase.) Tell them that there is no one correct answer; the idea is just to record the first thought that comes to them immediately after hearing the word.

When they have finished ten words or so, initiate a discussion on how different words mean different things to different people—not just a class of mixed foreign students, but all people even of the same culture. Our meanings or associations come from our past experiences and learnings. Ask a few students to share with the whole group their reaction to the first word you gave them. Talk about how our communication is diminished when our past experiences are not shared. Brainstorm how this problem could be lessened. How could we be more sure that we are being understood and that we are understanding others?

You might want to ask your students to each choose a partner and share their word reactions just to illustrate the point.

STRATEGY TYPE: Dyads
PERSONAL ☒ NON-PERSONAL ☐
TIME NEEDED: 10 minutes
MATERIALS: A preference handout

It's Your Choice

PROCEDURE:

Thought Gathering: Give each student a sheet with three or four topics on it. Ask each student to make an **X** by their first choice of an answer.

Sharing: With a partner, students will state their preference and offer some ideas on why they chose the way they did. This may be repeated with another partner.

Follow-up: As a follow-up, your students might want to take one topic and write a short composition on it.

Note: These choosing activities may pertain to a **particular topic** such as work, sex, leisure time, family and environmental concerns. Also, they may be created to conform to a **particular structure**, such as:

> I wish I could. . . .
> I wish I knew. . . .
> I wish I worked. . . .
> I wish I understood. . . .
> I wish I had. . . .

A preference sheet follows.

Variations on this activity have been presented many times at ESL conferences and conventions. Our thanks go to those who are probably the source of the idea behind these kinds of activities, Sidney Simon, Howie Kirschenbaum, and Leland Howe.
See resource guide in this book.

IT'S YOUR CHOICE

Where would you rather be on Saturday afternoon?

- ☐ Hiking in the mountains with a friend
- ☐ Sleeping in the sun in your backyard
- ☐ At a discount store with $50 to spend

Where would you rather live?

- ☐ A cabin in the mountains
- ☐ A big city
- ☐ On a farm
- ☐ In a small town

Which would you least like to do?

- ☐ Listen to a Beethoven concert
- ☐ Listen to a lecture on politics
- ☐ Listen to a debate on bi-lingual education

Which would you rather receive for your birthday?

- ☐ $10 to buy yourself something
- ☐ A gift worth $10
- ☐ A hand-made gift

STRATEGY TYPE: Dyads
PERSONAL ☒ **NON-PERSONAL** ☐
TIME NEEDED: 30/40 minutes
MATERIALS: 5"x7" index cards

Five By Sevens Focus

PROCEDURE:

Give each student a 5"x7" index card and ask them to write down words or phrases in answer to the questions you will ask. (Explain to them that it is not the writing that is important here. They are merely jotting down notes as reminders of the ideas that come to them so that they can be used for conversation.)

After the cards are filled (7 or 8 answers), ask them to form small groups where they can take turns around the circle sharing one answer at a time. Instruct the students to listen carefully without interruption to whomever is speaking. Have them go around the circle three or four times (one answer at a time for each person). Students are to choose who will go first and they will choose which answers they want to share. Some may be too personal or there may be questions they had no answer for! Set some sort of time limit and remind them when the time is half over so that they can judge if someone is taking up more than his or her share of the time.

It is suggested that areas that are "value rich," such as politics, religion, family, relationships, romance, work, leisure time, etc., be chosen when thinking up question for five by sevens. **Wh-** questions provide the most output. The following are some examples:

> Who gave you your first romantic kiss?
> Who is someone very special to you in your family?
> What was your first job?
> Name three things that you like about this town.
> Tell me three things that you can do very well.
> What book have you read that has influenced your life in some way?
> What is your religion? Is your religion an important part of your life?
> How do you spend most of your money?
> What do you like to do when you are alone?
> What is something you would like to change in your life?
> Where is a place you hope to visit someday?
> What is something you want to buy but you can't afford it yet?
> What makes you angry?
> Are you afraid of anything?
> Who is your "hero"?
> How do you spend your Saturday nights?
> What is a food that you just can't eat!?

Variations on this activity have been presented many times at ESL conferences and conventions. Our thanks go to those who are probably the source of the idea behind these kinds of activities, Sidney Simon, Howie Kirschenbaum, and Leland Howe.
See resource guide in this book.

STRATEGY TYPE: Dyads
PERSONAL ☒ **NON-PERSONAL** ☐
TIME NEEDED: 30 minutes
MATERIALS: Life cycle handout,
color crayons or water color pens

Life Cycle

PROCEDURE:

Distribute a life cycle handout to each individual. Divide the class into dyads.

Instructions:

1. Decide what the six most important events in your life have been.
2. Record the events on the life cycle chart.
3. Put your current age at the top of the chart.
4. Color each event a separate color
5. Label the events.
6. Exchange life cycle charts with your partner.

Consider the differences and similarities in your charts.

Consider the following questions:

1. How old were you when your first big event occurred?
2. Which events occurred the closest together?
3. Did you choose the colors for any particular reason? If yes, why?
4. Which event was the most recent?
5. Is there any event you remember better than the others? If yes, which one?
6. Do you notice anything similar about your chart and your partner's chart?
7. How long has it been since your last big event?
8. Do you notice differences in your chart and your partner's chart?
9. What difference do you notice?
10. Is any **one** event the most important?

LIFE CYCLE CHART

Example:

My current age is ___32___

Orange	I came to the United States
Red	
Blue	I had my first baby
	I got married
Green	I got my braces off
Yellow	
	I started school
Pink	My brother was born
Purple	My birth

Steps to follow:
1. Mark the events
2. Label events
3. Place colors

Personality Partners

PROCEDURE:

Divide students into pairs. Give them the following directions.

1. Write down five personality characteristics which make you different from anyone else. Write down the things which make you "you."

2. Now, turn to your partner and write down five characteristics which you discern from his/her physicial appearance, movements and facial expressions. Write down the things which make your partner who she/he is.

3. Exchange descriptions. Let your partner see what you have written. You will also want to see what she/he has written about you. Compare his/her description of you with the one you wrote of yourself.

Follow-up questions:

1. What surprises did you find?
2. What things did your partner write about you which **you** didn't write?
3. What things did you write which your partner didn't?
4. What things did you both write?
5. What did you learn about yourself?
6. Did you look for the same things in your partner you looked for in yourself?

Add Your Own!

5. Small group

Controversy

PROCEDURE:

At the beginning of class, post a piece of paper with a controversial statement written on it. Use large letters so that it can be seen from the back of the room. Say nothing about the statement. Let your students simply notice it accidentally. Twenty minutes before class is over ask your students to form groups of three or four. Tell them that you would like each student to make a statement or take a stand regarding the controversial sentence on the wall. Either agree or disagree and say why. Have each group decide who is going first. After the first person in the group has taken a stand, the second person must repeat exactly what the first person has said or restate it accurately (to the first person's satisfaction!) e.g., "You said you disagreed with the statement because . . . . . Is that right?" If the first person is not happy with the restatement, s/he asks the second person to try again until s/he is satisfied that his/her view has been well understood. Then person two takes a stand as the others listen. Then, the third person must repeat back or restate person two's position to his/her satisfaction, and so on until all three (or four) have had a chance to speak, be heard, and be understood. (This is a listening technique developed by Carl Rogers.)

Some sample controversial statements are given here, but invent your own, either in line with your students' current interests or regarding current news or events talked about in the newspapers or on T.V.

Marijuana should be legal and packaged commercially.

Immigration to the United States should be open and unlimited.

Homosexuality is immoral. All homosexuals should go to jail.

Abortion is a personal decision. The law and the church should stay out of it.

All drunk drivers should be sent to prison.

Parents should allow their teenage children to wear their hair any way they like and allow them to wear whatever clothes they like.

T.V. is a total waste of time. It makes people stupid.

Highschool cafeterias should not be allowed to sell junk food.

National pride is ridiculous. All borders and boundaries should be abolished.

Possessions

PROCEDURE:

Have students form groups of six. Tell them that this will be a chance to talk a bit about the things we have that are precious or important to us, things that give us pleasure, things we need, or things that we would hate to lose for some reason or another.

Choose any one of these topics and have each group take turns sharing answers around the circle.

"Something that I have in my pocket/purse that I always carry with me is.... because...."

"Something that I have in my bedroom that is very important to me is...."

"Something that my mother gave me...."

"Something I forgot to pack in my suitcase when I came to the United States (and I really need it!) is...."

"Something that I just bought...."

"Something that I have that I use all the time is...."

"Something that I have that makes me feel peaceful is...."

"Something that I have that makes me feel happy is...."

"Something I have that brings back memories is...."

Pictures, Pictures, Pictures

PROCEDURE:

Divide students into two or three groups with no more than five to a group. Each group will receive 20 pictures to pass around and look at. These should be a variety of pictures from magazines and should be mounted on 8½" x 11" colored construction paper. Each picture should be given a number or letter.

Instructions: Your group has just been given 20 pictures to pass around and look at. It will be the responsibility of your group to find things that these pictures have in common and place them in groups. Use your imagination and creativity. For example, let's say I have a picture of a bear, a cat, a dog, and an elephant. These pictures belong in the same group because they are all **animals.** This is something they all have in common. Appoint a secretary for the group. Have that individual write the number or letter of each picture which belongs in the group.

Make certain that each picture belongs in a group.

After each group has finished, ask them to come up to the front of the class and display their pictures by groups. The class must see if they can guess what the pictures have in common.

Make certain all class members understand **in common** and all the rules before the exercise begins.

For more ideas on this kind of activity, see Johnson, Leibig, Senatore, and Minor in our resource guide.

STRATEGY TYPE: Small Group
PERSONAL ☒ **NON-PERSONAL** ☐
TIME NEEDED: 15 minutes
MATERIALS: none

Thinking and Feeling

PROCEDURE:

In a large group have the students come up with a list of words which describe the feelings they have. Use the list on the following page if your students have difficulty in generating their own list. Check to see that all students understand the words which describe their feelings or emotions.

Divide students into small groups of three to five. Give each person a copy of the handout material below. Have each group find out how they feel at each of these times during the day. Each member of the group should be given a chance to share their feelings with the other group members. Stress active listening. After each person has had a chance to share, the group should be given about five additional minutes to discuss their differences and similarities.

Handout material:

How do you feel when . . . . .

1. you wake up
2. you get a good grade on a test?
3. you fight with a friend?
4. you don't get enough sleep?
5. someone gives you a present?
6. you get a bad grade on a test?
7. you receive letters from friends?
8. someone is cross with you?
9. you don't have any money?
10. you listen to music you like?

Use your imagination! Add other questions for your own class.

Some feelings I have . . . . .

accepted	bored	depressed
afraid	brave	disappointed
angry	calm	disgusted
ashamed	confident	enthusiastic
excited	high	intense
free	hopeful	jealous
good	hostile	joyful
guilty	hurt	lonely
happy	inadequate	loving
miserable	relieved	silly
nervous	resentful	strong
peaceful	sad	stubborn
puzzled	shaky	tender
rejected	shy	terrified
ugly	wonderful	
uptight	worried	
vulnerable		
warm		
weak		

STRATEGY TYPE: Small Group
PERSONAL ☒ **NON-PERSONAL** ☐
TIME NEEDED: 15 minutes
MATERIALS: none

Guided Fantasy

PROCEDURE:

Ask your students to find a comfortable position and relax, closing their eyes as you tell them a story. Tell them only to listen closely and imagine themselves in the scene. Select one of the open-ended "fantasies" and tell it very slowly, in a soft, clear voice with appropriate tonality to make the story realistic as possible. Embellish the story in any way you like, adding your own personal touches of creativity and using as many visual, auditory, kinesthetic, and olfactory (!) descriptions as you can in order to pull the students down into the story. After allowing your students two or three minutes to discover their own personal endings to the fantasy, have them form groups of three or four to share them with each other. No one should ever be compelled to share, only **allowed** to share. If it happens that only one or two want to speak in a group, that's okay; the others may just listen and comment. All may write their own personal endings in their journal or notebook.

Fantasy #1   The Gift Box

It is the end of the day. You have been really busy all day. Running. Thinking. Working. Hurrying. You're feeling a little tired, but it was a good day - satisfying and productive. You approach your house. You're really glad to be there where it is warm and comfortable and familiar. You reach out to the doorknob and take out your key. Where is it? Oh, here it is. You discover suddenly that the door is already unlocked! That's strange. You remember locking it this morning. You always lock it! You walk in. Everything looks the same, smells the same. Everything appears to be just as you left it. You take off your old jacket and throw it on the sofa. As you walk into the kitchen, you notice that there is a package on the table. A package? That's strange! It's all wrapped up like a present. What is this? What size is this gift? Very small? Very big? Look at the color of the paper. Notice the ribbon on top and the little note with your name on it. How curious! What could it be? Who could it be from? You sit down at the table running your hands over the paper; you're not sure that you want to open it. Oh well, go ahead. It's for you! You read the little note. It says, "Inside is a gift that you really want right now!" You slowly and carefully tear off the paper and the ribbons. You open the box and look inside. Wow! Look at that! That's wonderful! You are totally surprised. And look who it is from! How nice! Look over this gift for one minute and read the card inside again, and then share with your circle of friends just what you found in the box . . . . .

This is from a common psycho-therapy process.

Fantasy #2   A Message

It is a beautiful sunny Saturday morning in _____. You are sitting out in front of your home, relaxing in the sunshine and drinking your favorite early morning drink. The neighborhood is quiet. You look at the other houses on your street, the trees, the fences. You see that same dog that is always running around the streets. You look up and notice that there is a man on a bicycle coming down the street. He is wearing a green uniform and carrying a bag. He seems to be coming to your house. Yes, he sure is. You watch as he approaches your house. He stops his bicycle and gets off and walks up to you, calling your name. You say to him, "That's me!" He says that he is from Western Union Telegraph Service and that he has a very exciting telegram for you. He smiles and says how much he loves to deliver good news! He hands you the telegram with a wink and another smile. He says, "Sign here, please." You sign his paper and look over the yellow envelope. The delivery man rides off down the street on his bicycle. What can this be? Who is it from? Good news? You tear open the envelope and read the message. Your hands are shaking with excitement as you read the good news. You were sure hoping to get this news! Look over that note for one minute, then share with your group of friends what the message is and who it is from . . . . .

Fantasy #3   Magic Vitamins

You're feeling kind of blaah. Not sick. But not really well. Not sad, but not really happy. Not lazy, but not full of energy either. You're not really lonely, but it might be nice if someone visited you once in a while! You're just kind of in the middle. Your life isn't perfect now, but it isn't too bad. There is just a few things you would like to change, that's all. So, you decide to look for some help. You put on your jacket, open your door, leave your house and start walking. You walk and walk with nowhere special in mind. After a while, you find yourself on a street you never walked down before. You look into all sorts of different store windows. Something in a little red-painted shop catches your eye. You stop and look at the display in the window · vitamins · all kinds of vitamins. Vitamins you have never seen before, Vitamin HK, Vitamin Z and Vitamin X! What can these be for? You walk into the shop and pick up one bottle of each Vitamin · HK, X, and Z. You take them to the clerk and put them on the counter. "What are these vitamins for?" you ask him. "What do they do?" He tells you that these are special vitamins. Each one will change your life in some way, some good way. He asks you for $3.00.

You take your bottles of vitamins home and take one out of each bottle. By six o'clock that evening all three are starting to take effect. You are starting to feel really happy, really different with the changes that are beginning to happen in your life. These are truly wonderful vitamins. Experience these changes for one or two minutes, then tell your group what effect they are having on your life . . . . .

Fantasy #4   The Perfect Machine

On your kitchen table are various tools · a hammer, screw driver and screws, bolts, nuts, wire, wire cutters. On the table is a set of plans, too. You have worked and worked and finally have finished building your marvelous machine! Look it over. It is truly a fine invention. On the top you have put a small red button. On the back side is a little silver wheel. On the left side is a switch with a light in it that says on/off. On the right side you have added a lever that says, "pull me". In front there is a big crank. This is a very special little machine. You invented it. There is nothing like it in the whole world. Please make a picture of your machine for your group and tell them what happens when you flip the switch, push the button, turn the wheel, wind the crank, and pull the lever . . . . .

Fantasy #6   The Big Win

You are lying on your bed. It is not very comfortable. it feels hard and lumpy. You can't sleep. You're too cold. No, you're too hot. Throw off the blankets. No, pull them back up. You hear the noise of the traffic outside your window. You turn over again and again. The room is very dark. You wish you had someone to talk to. You have a hundred problems running through your head. Suddenly, in the middle of this terrible night, the telephone rings. You reach out in the darkness trying to find the telephone. Ooops! You dropped it on the floor. Where is it? Oh, here it is. "Hello?" A man's voice says, "Congratulations!! This is the Big Win Show on T.V. You have just won an all-expenses paid holiday anywhere in the world! Starting tomorrow at 8 o'clock in the morning you will be with any person you choose in any country or city you choose. You can stay for two days and do anything you like!" You have to decide in one minute where you would like to be and who you would like to be with. Think about your good luck for a minute and then share with your group how, where and with whom you will spend your ideal 48 hours . . . . .

Fantasy #7   The Wise Man

You are walking along a quiet beach. It is a cool, grey day. You breathe in the salt air and walk and walk and walk, watching the waves roll in and roll out. You have never been on this long, deserted beach before. You don't see any other people around. And that feels okay with you; you need time to be alone and just think about life. You listen to the singing of the sea birds and notice them flying across the very tops of the waves. You feel the sand collecting in your shoes. You finally come to a place where the rocks go out to the water's edge and you have to wait for the wave to go out before you can run around them to get to the other side. As the wave moves slowly back, you quickly run around the big rocks and continue to walk down the beach. Suddenly, you notice up ahead a dark opening in the wall of the cliff that towers along one side of the beach. You walk slowly towards it - and you peek inside. It is very dark and it looks like a big, black room, big enough to stand up in! You are curious. You slowly step inside and look deep into the darkness. You carefully walk deeper and deeper into the dark cave. Running your hands along the cool, damp wall, you try very hard not to fall in the blackness. You continue to walk slowly and carefully into the cave for a few more minutes. Funny, but you almost detect the smell of flowers . . . . roses, maybe. That's strange . . . . The wall takes a turn to the left, and as you round the corner you see a faint pink light glowing somewhere up ahead of you. A light? What can that be? Are you nervous in here? No . . . you feel fine . . . you feel very curious and you decide to keep walking toward the little light and the smell of roses. You step slowly and quietly and the light becomes brighter and clearer. You continue forward and then you feel the cave take another slight turn to the left. As you come around the turn in the wall, you find yourself face to face with an old, old man who is sitting on a large flat rock. His face is friendly and peaceful. His hair is long and pink-white. The light almost seems to be coming from his hair and body! He looks at you very calmly with a little smile - it seems as if he has been waiting for you. His eyes look directly into your eyes, and when he speaks, his voice is as soft as a cloud. "Have you come for your answer? I know you have come to me with a question . . . . " You look at his face and you know that he really could answer any question you might have. You know that he would be correct. There has been a very important question on your mind lately . . . you know that . . . maybe you could ask this old man and he could help you. He is patient. He smiles and waits for you to speak. Go ahead . . . ask him now and listen carefully to his wise answer and consider what it means to you. In a couple of minutes, maybe you would like to tell your group what the question was that you asked this old man and what sort of answer he gave to you . . . .

Finding Solutions

PROCEDURE:

General Procedures for Finding Solutions:

Thought Gathering: Pose the following problem to your students, giving them alternative solutions or giving them no ideas at all how to resolve it. Have them reflect quietly and individually on the problem and think of possible solutions and the consequences of the solutions.

You may wish to simply read the problem and ask them to take notes or you may provide written copies depending on the level and needs of your group.

Sharing: Ask your students to form groups of four or five and share their ideas on how the problem might be resolved. Give them five or ten minutes to discuss. Then have each group report to the larger group.

Here is a list of reminders for Finding Solutions. You may wish to share them with your class.

Guidelines for Finding Solutions

1. Describe the problem. Make certain everyone in the group understands.
2. Identify possible solutions. List them. Everyone in the group should have a chance to give a personal opinion.
3. Discuss the solutions. Decide what is wrong with them and what is right with them.
4. Agree on a solution as a group.
5. Be able to give two or three reasons why you feel it is the best solution.
6. Be prepared to share your solution with the class.

Guidelines for Individuals

1. Be an active listener!
2. Speak up so everyone can hear you.
3. Be sensitive to all group members.
4. Ask questions when you don't understand.
5. Stay on the subject of discussion.

Additional 'finding solutions' activities may be found in a small booklet published by NEA titled "Unfinished Stories for Use In The Classroom". Write NEA Publications, Sales Section, 1201 Sixteenth Street N.W., Washington DC 20036

Problem #1

Bill has always dreamed of becoming a lawyer. He has finally completed his bachelor's degree and has been accepted to law school. Law school will take another three years. If Bill makes it through law school, he will probably be able to get a job at about $35,000 per year with many opportunities for advancement and increases in his salary.

Bill is married to Sally. Unfortunately, Sally has become unexpectedly ill. She needs to have surgery. Sally and Bill have no insurance. The surgery is expensive - $3,500. Bill cannot afford to pay for the surgery. He also doesn't feel it's right to borrow the money without having a full-time job for the future.

Bill has been offered a job at a local business for $14,000. The job also provides an insurance plan so Sally's surgery would be paid for. The only problem with the job is that Bill would have to sign a contract for three years. Bill is now 27 years old. In three years, he would probably be too old to be admitted to law school.

What should Bill do? How should he solve this problem?

Problem #2

Karl's wife, Mary, is suffering from cancer. Without help, she may only have a few weeks to live. A drug, however, has been developed and is being used which could save her life. A druggist in Karl's hometown has the drug but is selling it for $2,000 in order to make a large profit. Karl does not have $2,000 to buy the drug and the druggist will not let him make a partial payment. He already owes money for his house and car and doesn't feel his bank will loan him anymore. Without the drug, Karl's wife will certainly die.

What should Karl do?

Problem #3

John's parents are sending him through school. They want him to study business; however, he does not want to study in that major. He wants to be a musician.

His parents have told him they will not pay for his education if he studies music. After a week of arguments, his parents have finally realized he is not interested in business. They have finally agreed to compromise and pay for his education if he only minors in music with a business major. What do you think John should do?

Problem #4

Ann was severely injured in an automobile accident last month. She has been in the hospital in a deep coma since the accident. Her doctors have said that there is no chance of Ann recovering because the damage to her brain is so extensive. Ann is being kept alive by machines. Her parents believe that keeping Ann alive with machines is wrong. She is nothing more than a vegetable. They believe she has a "right to die." They want to take Ann off the machines and allow her to die a natural death, quickly and with dignity. What should they do? What should the doctors do?

Questions to consider:

1. What does "the right to die" mean?

2. What does "death with dignity" mean?

3. What is **euthanasia**?

4. What is a coma?

Problem #5

Mark and Nancy Roberts have been married for six years. They have four children under the age of five. Nancy has recently had two miscarriages, and her doctor has informed her that the miscarriages are due to the fact that her body has never had time to recover from the four successful pregnancies. The doctor has suggested some form of birth control so that Nancy can regain her strength. He further suggested that perhaps four children were enough and that Nancy consider using a contraceptive indefinitely. He mentioned that perhaps John would like to come in and discuss a vasectomy. Nancy is also showing signs of strain in dealing with her four children - three of whom are still in diapers.

Mark is a pillar of his church. Part of his church doctrine indicates that "man should be fruitful and replenish the earth." He feels a moral responsibility to his God and his church community to produce as many children as he can. To prevent pregnancy is, Mark feels, against God's will, unnatural, and seeking the devil's pleasure. Mark loves his wife, Nancy, and his four children very much.

What should Mark and Nancy do?

Problem #6

Your best friend asks to borrow your favorite jacket just for one evening. He has a special date. You are a little reluctant; it is a very expensive jacket, and a gift from your father besides. But he **is** your best friend and you trust him. He brings the jacket back the next morning and thanks you for the loan. He says he felt terrific wearing it and his new girlfriend was really impressed. A few days later you take your jacket out of the closet and put it on and you notice that right in the front is a big cigarette burn - a big hole! Your heart just sinks! What do you do now? Can it be fixed? How much will it cost? What will your father say when he sees it? What can you say to your father? What will you say to your friend? Anything?

Problem #7

You are walking down Main Street; you are feeling really fine. You just got your paycheck and have bought three new record albums and got a haircut. Suddenly you are approached by a young man with longhair and dirty clothes who says, "Do you have any spare change? I am really hungry." He **looks** really hungry, and you **do** have some "spare" money right at this minute. What do you say to him?

Problem #8

You have planned to spend all afternoon just resting. You have had a really hard week and now you just want to take a long, slow bath, turn on some quiet music and read a good book. You deserve it! The phone rings. A good friend of yours asks you if you could donate three of your "delicious" chocolate cakes to the "bake sale" at the church which is tomorrow. You know that the church really needs money and relies on volunteers to help them out. She tells you that you have always been so wonderful, so conscientious and have helped them so much in the past, and that they were hoping they could count on you again. She says she hopes you are not too busy. **Are** you too busy? Do you say "yes" and spend all afternoon preparing cakes in the kitchen, or do you say "no, I'm sorry" and tell her that you are, in fact, very busy. Do you take the relaxing afternoon that you deserve?

Problem #9

Your mother has always been very conservative, but in the past few months she has been acting very strangely. She has started buying clothing that is really styled for teenagers - tight levis, bright colored halter tops and purple and green striped knee socks. She even bought a crazy hat with a penguin on the top. She seems to really enjoy wearing these clothes, but you think she looks terrible. You are afraid people will start to laugh at her. You love her very much, and you don't want to hurt her feelings, but, frankly, you are embarrassed to be seen with her lately! What will you do about this?

Problem #10

You go downtown with your best friend. As you walk through the drugstore, you see him/her pick up a pack of gum from a counter and put it in his/her pocket. You don't say anything, but you think it is a little strange. Later, as you are walking through the department store and looking at clothing, you see him/her pick up a pair of ski gloves and wrap them in his/her jacket. You walk out of the store and he/she doesn't pay for them. You think it is very wrong to steal. You also know there could be big trouble with the police. What do you do?

Problem #11

Your sister has written a poem. She really likes it. She thinks it is a wonderful poem! You think it is terrible. She wants your opinion. What do you tell her?

Tell her the truth - "I think it is not very good."

Tell her half of the truth - "Well, it's not bad; maybe it just needs a little more work."

Tell her what she wants to hear - "It is beautiful."

Brainteaser

PROCEDURE:

Divide students into groups of three to five. Give each group the following "brainteaser." Allow ten minutes for each group to find a solution. Encourage group discussion afterward.

Handout Material:

Who Married Carol?

Bill and Jane, Charlie and Francis, Frank and Carol, and Jim and Mary were all college sweethearts. Bill was engaged to Jane, but ended up with the woman who later became a model. Francis became a computer technician and married a college president who was not her college sweetheart. Mary became a teacher. Only one man married his college sweetheart. Who married Carol?

Consider the facts one at a time. Use the information below to help you. Cross out the names as the information is given.

Consider the following:

College sweethearts:

Bill and Jane
Charlie and Francis
Frank and Carol
Jim and Mary

Married partners:

Bill
Charlie
Frank
Carol

Partner possibilities:

Bill:	Jane	Francis	Carol	Mary
Charlie:	Jane	Francis	Carol	Mary
Frank:	Jane	Francis	Carol	Mary
Jim:	Jane	Francis	Carol	Mary

Notes to the teacher:

Use the information on the handout sheet. Follow the steps outlined below.

#1 Bill was engaged to Jane, but ended up with the woman who later became model. This means he did not marry Jane.

#2 Francis became a computer technician and married a college president who was not her college sweetheart. This means neither Bill nor Charlie married Francis. Bill married a model and Charlie and Francis were college sweethearts.

#3 Mary became a teacher. This means Bill did not marry her. Bill married Carol.

#4 Only one man married his college sweetheart. This means that Jim married Mary.

#5 Results: Jane married Charlie
Bill married Carol
Frank married Francis
Jim married Mary

#6 Who married Carol?

Answer: Bill married Carol

#7 Go through this procedure with the students. Let them supply the answers. Allow time for thought gathering and discussion.

STRATEGY TYPE: Small Group
PERSONAL □ **NON-PERSONAL** ☒
TIME NEEDED: 10 minutes
MATERIALS: Black board and chalk

Word Search

PROCEDURE:

Divide the class into groups of three to five. Write a polysyllabic English word on the board, i.e., **Encyclopedia** or **Translation.**

Instructions: I have just written the word _____ on the board. Your group will now have three minutes to make as many words as possible from the letters in this word. Possible words from **Encyclopedia**, for example, would be **can, an, loan,** and **pedal.** Words from **Translation** would be **train, sit, rat,** etc. (Write examples on board). Your group will receive a score equal to the number of correct words. Each group should have a secretary. Only the secretary can write words within the group. If you think of a word the the group secretary and s/h will write it down. Your group may challenge any of the other groups for correct words. If you do not believe the word they have is correct, you say **challenge.** Look up the word in the dictionary. If you do **not** find the word, you get their point. If you find the word, they get the point.

Create A Story

PROCEDURE:

Prepare a set of sixteen cards for each group of four students. On each card is written one word. Each set is identical. Theoretically, any words are okay to use, but we suggest:

came	family	hope	try
found	different	love	wait
happiness	never	can	always
best	money	future	decide

Have your students form groups of four and give each group a set of cards. Shuffle the cards and deal them out. Ask students to put their cards on the table in front of them and choose who will go first. The first person will make a sentence containing one of his or her words. Anyone, then, can add the next line or lines to the narrative using one of his/her words to begin forming a (relatively) cohesive story. Continue adding lines with students using words from their cards until all words are included and the story is complete. (In order to make the story hold together, students may have to use as many as thirty or more lines.)

Variation:

After their story has been done orally, have the group appoint a "secretary" who will write down the story as the group retells it. These written stories could be shared with the larger group in order to see how the stories differ. Or the large group sharing could be done orally as well.

STRATEGY TYPE: Small Group
PERSONAL ☐ **NON-PERSONAL** ☒
TIME NEEDED: 20 minutes
MATERIALS: Sample story handout

News Stories

PROCEDURE:

Give a sample news story to each student. A story similar to the following can be used:

News Story

Facts: Bank robbery at 2:00 p.m.
           The bank robber was seen leaving the bank by Mr. James.

           Mr. James was shot in the leg.

           The get-a-way car was seen by Mrs. Petersen. She was hit by the car in the parking lot. She was not seriously injured.

           The bank tellers, Miss Anderson and Mr. Wilson, talked with the robber.

           The policeman also got a close look at him.

Choose students from the class to play the five parts: Mr. James, Mrs. Petersen, Miss Anderson, Mr. Wilson, and the policeman. Assign a news reporter to each person. Have the reporters interview that person for three to five minutes to find out the details of the robbery. Students use their imaginations in answering. It is helpful to use a small bell or whistle to indicate when the time is up.

Each news reporter should have a copy of example questions.

Example questions:

      1. What color were the robber's eyes?

      2. What color was his hair?

      3. What kind of gun did he have?

      4. What was he dressed in?

      5. How tall was he?

      6. How much did he weigh?

      7. Did he have any unusual characteristics?

      8. What did his car look like?

      9. Was he alone?

    10. In which direction did he leave?

When all reporters have interviewed the people involved, give them five minutes to organize their information.

Follow-up activity:

Have Students bring in real news items and write their own stories.

Notes to the teacher:

The sample stories need to be written with your specific class in mind. The Bank Robbery used five people and five reporters, a total of ten. If you had a larger class you would expand the story somewhat in order to include all students in the class.

STRATEGY TYPE: Small Group
PERSONAL ☐ **NON-PERSONAL** ☒
TIME NEEDED: 20 minutes
MATERIALS: Handouts

Starting Over

PROCEDURE:

Divide your students into groups of three to five. Give each student a copy of the following handout. Tell each group that they must find a solution.

Handout Material:

News Flash—The civilized world has been destroyed by mysterious moon-rays. Ten people have managed to find shelter and have survived. The shelter has enough food, etc. to sustain seven adult people until it is safe to return to the earth's atmosphere. On the basis of what you think society would need to survive, make a list of seven ideal people who would help the human race start over.

Consider the following:

1. What are their names?
2. How old are they?
3. What occupations should they have?
4. Do they have any physical limitations?
5. Can they produce children?

6. What are their political views?
7. What are their religious views?
8. What are their educational backgrounds?
9. What is the racial balance?

Write a description and give facts for each one.

Follow-up activities:

I. After the groups have come up with a list of seven survivors, have them share their information with the rest of the class by writing the names on the board and having certain group members provide the information on each survivor. Encourage questions.

II. As a follow-up activity you may also wish to record each group's results and compare the following day.

Consider the following:

1. What occupations did each group use?
2. What occupation did your group feel was important which another group did not?
3. Could all groups produce children?
4. What were the ages of the survivors?
5. What religions were accounted for, if any?
5. What is the racial balance?

Picture Solving

PROCEDURE:

Divide your students into groups of three to five each. Give each student two pictures. Each picture should be mounted and numbered. each group should make five questions for each picture. The questions should be specific. Have each group appoint a secretary who can write the questions as the group agrees on them. Only one person in the group should write. The group must decide **together** what questions to ask.

Follow-up:

1. What questions could have been asked about more than one picture?

2. What questions did you have a hard time answering?

3. Did you have a favorite picture? Why or why not?

4. How did your group work?

5. Did anyone talk too much?

6. Did anyone need to talk more?

The Desert Island

PROCEDURE:

For this activity your students will have to understand the ideas **pretend** or **make believe.** You may wish to use a simple activity to demonstrate these words before beginning this exercise. Hand out the list of items which follows. Read the following paragraph to your class.

Instructions:

Pretend you are on a sinking ship. There are rubber boats available for your rescue. The boats can hold only a limited amount of supplies and people. You can see a small desert island in the distance. If your boat makes it there safely, you will need things to help you survive until you're rescued.

Look at the list of items you have been given. You can take only three items from each group. Divide into groups of three to five. Your group must decide together which things to take and which things to leave behind. You cannot decide individually.

Remember! Everyone in your group must agree.

Teacher notes:

Make certain all students understand before beginning the activity. Depending on the level of your group you may have to read the story and instructions several times. Discuss the vocabulary items on the handout material if necessary.

For more ideas on this kind of activity, see Johnson, Leibig, Senatore, and Minor in our resource guide.

Group 1	**Group 2**	**Group 3**
Large flares	Pillows	Fresh water
Matches	Sleeping bags	7-up
Flashlights	Tent	Coffee
Oil lamps	Blankets	Canned juices
Oil	Sheets	Beer
Batteries	Coats and jackets	Tea
Can opener	Extra clothes	Whiskey
Utensils		

Group 4	**Group 5**	**Group 6**
Salt	Bows and arrows	Frozen meat
Flour	Set of knives	Dried fruits
Sugar	Gun	Dried vegetables
Yeast	Bullets	Fresh fruits
Dry milk	Fishing pole	Fresh vegetables
Water purification tablets	Small chairs	Canned beans
	Dishes	Dry soup
	First-aid kit	
	Ropes	

Follow-up:

In a large group find out why the groups chose to select the items they did and why they left others behind.

Changes in Meaning

PROCEDURE:

Give the following demonstration to your students. Consider these words:

She's not home.

Call on the students to say them in different ways.

1. with anger
2. with apology
3. with question
4. with sadness

Make the point that it is not **what** we say, but **how** we say it that is important.

Divide students into small groups. Supply them with the following handout material. Explain the five different types of statements people use. Ask them to consider each sentence and try to think of the different ways the statement may be interpreted. Also, have them consider the circumstances wherein the statement may be said.

Handout materials:

Different types of statements

Future Statement: Deals with the future

Command Statement: Gives a command or a directive to do something

Experience Statement: Gives information

Rule Statements: Follow a particular rule

Private Statements: Show personal feelings or opinions

Discuss the following statements in your groups and decide where they belong. Mark the sentences and then organize them into groups. Sentences may belong to more than one group. Use the following abbreviations.

Abbreviations:

Future Statement = FS

Command Statement = CS

Experience Statement = ES

Rule Statement = RS

Private Statement = PS

Kinds of Statements

1. There are 365 days in a year.
2. Bill's mother has blonde hair.
3. Sue is a pretty girl.
4. I am going to Mexico next summer.
5. Sit down.
6. Pull your chairs in a circle.
7. It's five o'clock.
8. If you will open the windows, you'll feel better.
9. The movie begins at 9 o'clock.
10. Smoking cigarettes causes lung cancer.
11. It costs 18 cents to send a letter in the United States.
12. The papers are in the office.
13. The book is brown.
14. Add 1 teaspoon of flour.
15. Your coat is dirty.
16. If you'd wash your car, it would look better.
17. He was born in 1949.
18. Thirty-six inches make 1 yard.
19. I have a headache.
20. I like your new suit.

Add Your Own!

6. Large group

STRATEGY TYPE: Large Group
PERSONAL ☐ **NON-PERSONAL** ☒
TIME NEEDED: 45 minutes
MATERIALS: large newsprint or butcher paper "charts" and 4 faces cut from a magazine

The Ideal Partner

PROCEDURE:

Hang large 'charts," each one having a picture of a face cut from a magazine. Give each face a first name and a list of character traits or qualities.

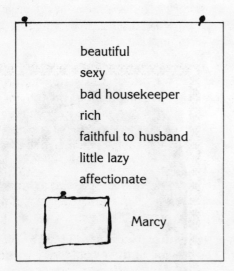

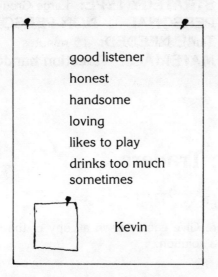

good listener
honest
handsome
loving
likes to play
drinks too much
sometimes

Kevin

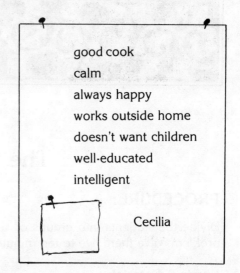

good cook
calm
always happy
works outside home
doesn't want children
well-educated
intelligent

Cecilia

Read the charts together and discuss the types of persons. What are their "good" qualities? What are qualities that might be hard to live with? Have a general discussion of who they would personally choose for a husband or wife. Try to get them to explain briefly why.

Then, divide the class up with the men in one room, the women in another. Have each group work together to brainstorm a list of qualities that they find important in a prospective partner. After 15 minutes, bring the two groups back together and have them share each others' lists. Find out what the men think of the women's list. Is it fair? Are the things they chose really important? Is there something that is missing from the list as far as they are concerned? Are they surprised to see what the women wrote or was it very predictable? Then have the women evaluate the men's list in the same way.

Next, if interest is still high, you might want to have each individual choose the **three** most important characteristics they look for in a mate and rank order them. After a couple of minutes, take a tally of both men and women to see if there is any consensus.

Finally, you could ask your students to consider the list of characteristics in a different perspective. Of the most important qualities listed, how many of them could they ascribe to themselves personally? Rather, if Luis says he thinks it is important for his partner to be neat and organized, honest, a good listener, and crazy about children, does he, himself fit these characteristics? Are we looking for a partner who is exactly like we ourselves are? Or are we looking for someone who is very different from us, someone who would complement us?

The Horse Traders

PROCEDURE:

Divide the students into groups of seven to ten. Give each person a copy of the following problem. Give them five to ten minutes to find a solution.

Handout Material:

Mr. Jones originally bought his horse, Charlie, for $300.00. He sold him to Mr. Smith for $350.00. Mr. Smith gave him $300.00 in cash with the promise that he would pay the remaining $50.00 within a month. Before Mr. Smith could pay Mr. Jones, he sold Charlie to Peter for $350.00. Peter gave Mr. Smith $250.00 with the promise to pay the $100.00 balance soon. Mr. Jones then wanted to buy Charlie back. He offered Peter $300.00. Peter accepted. Peter was happy because he made $50.00 and Mr. Jones had his horse back for the same price he paid in the first place.

Is Mr. Jones correct? Is Peter correct? What about Mr. Smith? What is wrong with the final result of this story? Find the answers to these questions. Use the following materials to help you.

Consider these questions:

1. Who should be happy with the final horse trading?

_____ Mr. Jones

_____ Mr. Smith

_____ Peter

2. Who should disagree with the final horse trading?

_____ Mr. Jones

_____ Mr. Smith

_____ Peter

3. Who owes money?

_____ Mr. Jones

_____ Mr. Smith

_____ Peter

STRATEGY TYPE: Large Group
PERSONAL ☐ **NON-PERSONAL** ☒
TIME NEEDED: 15 minutes
MATERIALS: Large bag and 1 personal
item from each student

Grab Bag

PROCEDURE:

Ask each student in the class to bring a small personal item to class. Tell them what they bring should be a secret. They should not let anyone else in the class know what they are bringing. It's a good idea to tell the students to bring items which are small and which will not break. Show them an average size grocery sack and tell them that all the items from the class must fit in the bag. After you have collected one item from every individual in the class, you are ready to start the activity. (Sometimes it takes several days to get **one** item from everyone so plan ahead!) Have a volunteer student come up to the front of the class and pick out an object and show it to the class. The class will offer suggestions as to whose object it is and why they believe it is true. After one or two minutes of discussion the student who drew the item should find out if the class was correct.

Keeping Journals

PROCEDURE:

1. In order to do this activity, students will have to make journals as a classroom activity. These can be made simply and inexpensively by cutting 15 (8½"x 11") pieces of paper in half and stapling the pages together in book form. Have students decorate their covers. On the days you use the exercise, give each student his or her own journal and a copy of the handout questions.

Journal Questions:

1. Where were you born?

2. Where have you lived during your life?

3. How long have you been in America?

4. Where would you want to live if you could live anywhere in the world?

5. How many brothers and sisters do you have?

6. Tell us about your parents.

7. Are you married? Do you have children?

8. Do you want to marry? How many children do you want to have?

9. What are you studying? Do you enjoy studying?

10. What is your occupational goal?

11. What are your hobbies?

12. What sports do you enjoy?

13. Are you a religious person? What is your religion?

14. What is your favorite food? Do you like American food?

15. What are your political views?

16. What do you think about America?

17. What languages do you speak?

18. What do you do for fun?

19. What do you enjoy talking about?

20. Do you enjoy music? What kind of music do you enjoy?

21. Do you play a musical instrument?

2. Explain that the journal will be a record of their classmates and that during the next two weeks they will all interview each other. All information will be recorded in the journal.

3. Have them write the names of their classmates in the journal, one name on each page.

4. Divide them into pairs. Give them 8-10 minutes for the first interview. Each person must have a chance to ask and answer questions. Make certain they write the information.

5. After 8-10 minutes, have students switch partners.

Follow-up Activity

In a large group, have the students share the information they found out about their classmates. Encourage them to ask questions when they don't understand or when they want more information.

Notes to the teacher:

1. Two eight to ten-minute interviews each class period work well. Use the activity until all students have interacted.

2. Follow each interview with five minutes of large group sharing.

3. Collect the journals and questions each day.

4. Let students know you will read the journals because you are interested. We have found it a good idea to write comments but not to correct.

5. Gently remind the students to be active listeners.

Five Good Minutes

PROCEDURE:

Ask your students to think over how they have spent the last 24 hours—where they have been, who they have seen, what types of activities have they been involved in. Give them a couple of minutes to gather their thoughts, and think of five good minutes that they really enjoyed. Five minutes that really bring us pleasure is often something hard to find! Whip around the room quickly having each student briefly share with the class their "five good minutes" as you jot them down in a list on the board.

When the list is complete, have the group try to determine just exactly what are the factors involved in our enjoyment—what kinds of things tend to make our life worth while. (Common factors are music, books, friends, sports, romance, rest, sports, praise.) See if the categories break down culturally. (They probably won't—and that is a lesson in itself in universality!) Initiate a discussion with the students regarding how they could get more of these good minutes into their lives. Realistically speaking, what would they have to do or what would the circumstances have to be in order to experience more of this enjoyment? Do they foresee this happening in the future? Why? Why not?

Families and Homelife

PROCEDURE:

Divide the class into groups of 8-12. Give each student a copy of the handout material. Explain to the groups the topic of discussion (in this case families and homelife). Each group is instructed to find out what experiences the members have had. A secretary should be appointed to record a summary. Remind students of the criteria for successful group discussion. (See Guidelines for Finding Solutions on page 72).

Handout Materials:

Group Questions

1. Who did most of the domestic chores in your home?
2. Did your mother work outside the home?
3. Were you given assigned duties each day? If yes, what were they?
4. Do you remember being punished for doing things wrong? If yes, how?
5. Did you have a lot of manufactured toys?
6. What was your favorite toy as a child?
7. Do you remember receiving bedtime lullabies or songs? If yes, do you remember them?
8. Did you have bedtime stories?
9. Do you remember being read to at other times?
10. Was some sort of religious prayer offered at mealtimes?
11. Was religion an important part of your family life?
12. Did your father return home for the mid-day meal? Did you after school age?

After 10 minutes of questions, stop the groups. Pass out summary sheets. Allow 10 more minutes for students to collect their summary sheet results.

Group Summary Sheet

I. Work at home

1. What were the domestic chores done in your group?

2. How often were they done?

3. How many mothers worked outside the home?

II. Religion

1. How important was religion in your group?

2. Were prayers at night common?

3. Did your group generally offer prayers at mealtime?

4. Did your group members eat the mid-day meal at home?

III. Bedtime

1. How many members had lullabies or songs at bedtime?

2. How many members had bedtime stories?

3. Would anyone like to share a song or lullaby?

4. How many in your group remember having stories read to them?

Follow-up

Have each group share their results with the entire class.

Upsies and Downsies

PROCEDURE:

(Allow time for thought gathering.)

Give the following explanation to the group:

An "upsy" is something or someone who has made you feel good. (Give an example.)
A "downsy" is something or someone who has made you feel bad. (Give an example.)

1. Recall someone who was an "upsy" for you. Think about the way the person made you feel. If you would like to, share your thoughts with the group.

2. Recall someone who was a "downsy" for you. Think about the way the person made you feel. If you would like to, share your thoughts with the group.

3. Think about the last time you were an "upsy" for someone else. What did you do? How did you feel? What did they do? How did they feel? If you would like to, share your thoughts with the group.

4. Think about the last time you were a "downsy" for someone else. What did you do? How did you feel? What did they do? How did they feel? If you would like to, share your thoughts with the group.

5. Think about **things** which have been "downsies" for you. If you would like to, share them with the group.

6. Think about **things** which have been "upsies" for you. If you would like to, share them with the group.

Notes to the teacher:

1. Give plenty of time for thought gathering.

2. Encourage students to ask questions of each other.

3. Share your own experiences first. Give examples.

4. Make a list of **things** which are "upsies" and "downsies." Write them on the board. Then proceed to personal experience sharing.

STRATEGY TYPE: Large Group
PERSONAL ☐ **NON-PERSONAL** ☒
TIME NEEDED: 10 minutes
MATERIALS: Blackboard and chalk

The Idea Blizzard

PROCEDURE:

Have your class as a whole brainstorm as many ideas as they can come up with of things to do in their new (American) hometown that are fun and entertaining and cost less than $4.00. Accept **all** ideas, no matter how crazy. Ask a secretary to jot them down on the board.

When a list has been made, ask various students whether they have ever done these things or if they would like to. See which activity interests which students. Suggest to your students that they make a social calendar for their class in order to organize outings together. Make a list of students' names and phone numbers. Find out who has a car and who doesn't, and who is over 21. (For dancing in clubs!) This is an excellent way to encourage your students to become socially active together and practice their new language out of the classroom.

Variations on this activity have been presented many
times at ESL conferences and conventions. Our thanks
go to those who are probably the source of the idea
behind these kinds of activities, Sidney Simon, Howie
Kirschenbaum, and Leland Howe.
See resource guide in this book.

STRATEGY TYPE: Large Group
PERSONAL ☒ **NON-PERSONAL** ☐
TIME NEEDED: 20 minutes
MATERIALS: Two character sketches that represent opposite points of view

Polar Opposites—By Degree

PROCEDURE:

In one corner of the room set up a "character", either a photo or a drawing of a person or yourself. Then, describe an extreme, detailed stance on a particular topic. (See ideas below for assistance.)

In the opposite corner of the room, define another "character", using a different photo or picture or another person who holds a viewpoint that is absolutely contrary to the first stance. After students have had a chance hear the two extremes, have them picture an imaginary line down the center of the room, running from pole to pole. Ask them to stand somewhere on the "line" according to where their own particular philosophy on the topic might place them. In order for them to decide just where to stand, it will be necessary for them to consult with each other. When the line has formed and the students think they are where they should be, ask four or five students to share their stances. See if they can tell you any specific past experiences or current circumstances that may have caused them to choose their position on the line.

This activity lends itself well to any controversial topic or any subject where the opposites can be easily defined. Some topic ideas you might want to try are:

    T.V. fanatic vs. T.V. hater

    Avid letter-writer vs. Non-letter-writer

    Family and friend person vs. Hermit

    Quick, hot-tempered person vs. Calm, cool, and collected

    Very religious vs. Atheist

    Clothes horse vs. Wardrobe ascetic

    Studying fool vs. Never studies

    Health food nut vs. Junk food addict

In this activity, it is imperative to build up the character sketches to the extreme or exaggerated point of view so that students have a clear picture of what they are or are not identifying with. The following examples will help you understand how a character might be portrayed.

A. Plug-It-In-Paul is crazy for electrical appliances and gadgets. In his bedroom alone he has an electric clock, a radio, an electric blanket, and a bed that gives a massage with just the flip of a switch. In addition, he has an automatic pajama folder, and a closet door that is operated by an electric eye. He pushes a button, and an electric current opens and closes the drawers in his dresser. He has automatic curtain pulls, electric carpet (heated) and a fancy electric page-turner for reading in bed without having to take his hands out from under the electric blanket. His pillow turns automatically every 23 minutes, and when it is time to get up in the morning, he is awakened by the eletronic melodies produced by two Moog synthesizers . . .

B. Back-To-Nature-Nancy cooks over an open fireplace. She entertains herself at night by playing checkers by a kerosene lamp and listening to her canary sing. She keeps her milk cold in an old Coleman ice chest and wouldn't dream of drying her hair any other way but in the sunlight. She has a wind-up clock, an old Schwinn Cruiser bicycle to take her to work at the local feed and grain, and she doesn't own an iron . . .

Follow up the group-sharing portion of "Polar Opposites" with dyad sharing, having students pair up with someone from the opposite end of the line. Also, they might want to try a short writing exercise based on their immediate learnings.

STRATEGY TYPE: Large Group
PERSONAL ☐ NON-PERSONAL ☒
TIME NEEDED: 15 minutes
MATERIALS:

Choosing Sides

PROCEDURE:

Each student will be given a chance to consider two opposite symbols and will be asked to choose which one best describes him/her. You might ask your students, for example, Are you an old Volkswagen or a new Datsun 240Z? Direct all the VW's to the left side of the room, and the Datsuns to the right. Each student must make a choice—nobody may stay in the middle of the room. When sides are taken, ask three or four volunteers from each side of the room to express why they chose as they did. Use questions such as:

What's it like to be a . . . . . .?

How do you know that you are a . . . . . .?

How does it feel to be a . . . . . .?

Tell me about . . . . . .?

Are you glad you are a . . . . . .? Why

How long have you been a . . . . . .?

What's the advantage to being a . . . . . .?

For each time you present this activity, give them three or four different sets of symbols in a row, so that they will have an opportunity to move back and forth across the room, associating with different students according to their choice of symbols. With each set presented, elicit responses from different students, using the types of process questions listed above.

Variations on this activity have been presented many
times at ESL conferences and conventions. Our thanks
go to those who are probably the source of the idea
behind these kinds of activities, Sidney Simon, Howie
Kirschenbaum, and Leland Howe.
See resource guide in this book.

As a follow up to this exercise, students might like to form dyads or small groups and continue sharing in depth their opinions or feelings brought up by the exercise. Possibly they might want to make some sort of statement in writing about the things they thought or discovered about each other during the activity.

Other ideas for choosing sides might be:

Are you a

Why or a why not?

Watch-it-done or a do-it-yourself?

Loud speaker or a private phone?

Screen door or an open window?

Pussy cat or a tiger?

Dancing shoe or a jogging shoe?

Sunrise or a sunset?

Throw-it-away-and-buy-a-new-one or a fix-up-the-old-one?

Cold shower or a hot tub?

Wall Street Journal or a comic book?

Do-it-now or an it-can-wait?

Champagne-and-the-Hilton or beer-and-camping?

Make-a-list or a where-am-I?

White gloves or dusty boots?

Add Your Own!

Resource Guide

Alexander, L.G. <u>For and Against</u>. Longman, Inc.

An oral practice book for advanced students designed to develop skills in discussion and debate. Topics for discussion are presented in a statement supported by an essay. Each is followed by a summary of the argument and counter argument. The material is designed to be very flexible and can be used for a wide range of aural/oral exercises.

Alexander, L.G., R. Kingsbury and J. Chapman. <u>Take A Stand</u>. Discussion topics for adult intermediate students. Longman, Inc.

It focuses on controversial topics that appeal to the adult learner. Thirty topics are presented through debate notes, editorial letters, well-known comic strips and other interesting means of beginning conversation.

Alexander, L.G., M.C. Vincent, and J. Chapman. <u>Talk It Over</u>. Discoussion topics for adult intermediate students. Longman, Inc.

It consists of 30 contemporary discussion topics. Introductory material (dialogs, letters, cartoons, charts, newspaper articles and photographs) and exercises to guide the student from controlled discussion to open-ended debate.

Allen, Edward David and R.M. Valette. <u>Classroom Techniques</u>. Foreign Languages and English as a Second Language. Harcourt Brace Jovanovich.

The purpose of this handbook is to show instructors ways of using, and adding to existing materials for the teaching of ESL. The text includes hundreds of examples and illustrations that may be directly applied in the classroom to improve communicative competence. A final section in the book suggests ways of teaching culture—both general civilization and patterns of daily life.

Ballard, Jim. <u>Circlebook</u>. A leader handbook for conducting "circletime," a curriculum of affect. Mandala Publishers.

This is essentially a set of guidelines for developing affective growth and human relationships and skill development. It has 15 pages of conversation topics.

Black, Colin. <u>A Handbook of Free Conversation</u>. Oxford University Press.

This book outlines a planned approach to free conversation and includes materials for 17 interesting classroom discussions.

Blot, Dave and P.B. Sher. <u>Getting Into It: an unfinished book</u>. New York Language Innovations.

A collection of 13 short essays with problematic endings. Each story deals with a socio-cultural problem experienced by an ESL student in the United States. Readers are invited to brainstorm possible solutions to each problem, drawing from their own personal experiences.

Boyd, John R. and M.A. Boyd. <u>Alice Blows a Fuse: Fifty Strip Stories in American English</u>. Prentice Hall.

This workbook engages students in communication and interaction in the ESL classroom. It combines exposure to natural language, survival situations and the strip story method of instruction. It contains 50 chapters with a strip story. Each story is followed up with reinforcement activities and exercises.

Byrd, Donald R.H. and I. Clemente-Cabetas. <u>React Interact Situations for Communications</u>. Regents Publishing Co.

It is composed of 22 situations to stimulate real communication and expand vocabulary and grammar. The text develops the communicative functions of giving information and advice, persuading others, expressing preferences, opinions, reasons, and feelings. Each lesson contains questions for oral interaction, exercises for written reaction, and a vocabulary list with definitions.

Byrne, Donn. <u>Progressive Picture Compositions</u>. Longman, Inc.

Twenty-six compositions for oral and written work. The theme of each composition is illustrated by a progressive series of four pictures. The pictures are spiralbound in four sets. The pictures are also reproduced in the Student's Book which provides guided written exercises for each composition.

Byrne, Donn and Andrew Wright. <u>What Do You Think? Picutres for Free Oral Expression</u>. Longman, Inc.

Designed to stimulate free oral expression, these books consist entirely of photographs and illustrations. The Teacher's Books provide detailed guidance for using the visual situations presented in the Student's Books, and the material is geared to helping students express themselves both in public and in their personal lives.

Carver, Tina Kasloff and S.D. Fotinos. <u>Conversation Book: English in Everyday Life</u>. Prentice Hall.

A conversational text for beginning or intermediate ESL students features a non-academic approach. Encourages students to talk about themselves in their own words. Uses practical situations and focuses each chapter on a separate aspect of everyday life—health, home, employment, etc. Offers a variety of open-ended conversational exercises—circle games, questions, role playing, conversation matrices, demonstration questions. Contains writing assignments at different levels, tied into various topics. Includes over 900 humorous illustrations.

Chamberlin, Anthony and K. Stenberg: Consulting Editors, L. Schinke and M. Siedlitz. <u>Play and Practice</u>. High-interest games and activities for ESL students of all ages! National Textbook Company.

A collection of 98 games for students of all levels and ages. Each activity is identified by objective. Games are graded by difficulty. The table of contents lists the nature of each game and the level for which it is best suited. They are suitable for individual play, play in pairs, and play in small, medium, or king-sized groups.

Chenfield, Mimi Brodsky. <u>Teaching Language Arts Creatively</u>. Harcourt Brace Jovanovich.

It covers all facets of the language arts curriculum, including listening, speaking, movement and drama, literature, reading, writing, and skills development. The text shows how instructors may draw upon their own experiences to improve their teaching. It also provides hundreds of practical ideas and activities for the classroom and challenges instructors to devise their own.

Coleman, Bruce and J. Hileman. <u>Coming to America</u>. Newbury House

26 student projects are followed by exercises in reading, dialogue, and writing. Can be used as a springboard for discussion.

Dixson, Robert J. <u>Exercises in English Conversation</u>. Regents Publishing Co.

This two-book series uses direct method techniques and introduces grammar through conversation practice. Each lesson has a dialogue or short reading, oral exercises, and a review.

English Language Service. <u>Readings and Conversations About the United States, its History and its Customs</u>. English Language Service.

Contains 20 lessons. Ten lessons are introduced by a reading passage, and ten lessons by a conversation. The lessons include fluency practices, vocabulary study, discussion topics, and writing exercises. In reading lessons subject matter is presented in a literary style like that which students will encounter in reading books and journals. In conversatio lessons, an opportunity to discuss lesson topics in guided, colloquial conversations is provided.

Ferreira, Linda A. and M. Vai. <u>Read On, Speak Out</u>! Newbury House Publishers.

This reader can be used as a basis for drawing advanced students into communication about stimulating contemporary issues. It has ten study units. Students are involved in discussion of the pros and cons of specific positions on these issues. The use of anaogies as measurement-exercises throughout the program reinforces integrated competency in all major aspects of English language use.

Finocchiaro, Mary. <u>Let's Talk</u>. Regents Publishing Co.

An effective medium for developing conversational fluency. A useful feature of the book is that some dialogues are brief conversational exchanges while others are sustained dialogues. It covers many situational themes and includes a special section for use with young children.

Flynn, Elizabeth and John LaFaso. <u>Group Discussion As a Learning Process</u>. Pennant Books.

Sourcebook: An excellent sourcebook for group discussion leadership. Provides paractical assistance and management tips for anyone who conducts group discussions. Offers suggestions for possible problems that can develop within the group: communication, lack of participation, conflicts, driting from the subject, etc. Provides group organizational suggestions.

Guidebook: Provides examples of applying ideas and techniques explored in the Sourcebook: Offers exercises that help students function effectively and productively as group members. Encourages appropriate formulation and use of questions in the learning process.

Ford, Carol K. and A.M. Silverman. <u>American Cultural Encounters</u>. Alemany Press, Ltd.

Presents situations for student discussion, thought and activities to emphasize American cultural practices and awareness of American culture. 50 problem situations are presented and possible solutions discussed. For intermediate and advanced ESL students in adult, college or secondary.

Graham, Carolyn, <u>Jazz Chants</u>. Oxford University Press.

This is a collection of chants and poems which sets everyday situational English to jazz rhythms to demonstrate the rhythm and intonation pattern of conversational American English.

Graham, Carolyn, <u>Jazz Chants for Children</u>. Oxford University Press.

Uses chants, songs, and poems to teach conversational American English to elementary school children. It capitalizes on children's natural affinity for rhyming, games, rhythm, and movement in a systematic series of units focusing on their emotional as well as linguistic needs. Each unit consists of a chant, song, or poem which teaches the basic structure of the chant. Chants dealing with feelings such as anger, fear, joy, pride, and many others are presented with accompanying picture activities such as puzzles, mazes, and matching games.

Grosset, Phillip. <u>Link Up</u>. Evans Books. Delta System

A collection of source material for discussion, of real interest and relevance to advanced students. Using a range of contrasting materials, such as cartoons, comic strips and photographs, the book follows man's life from before birth to after death, through childhood, adolescence, getting a job, forming relationships and growing old, and considers issues such as factory farming, patriotism, science fiction, the media and belief in God. There are newspaper articles, cartoons, advertisements and poems to make discussions lively and informed.

Grosset, Phillip. <u>Things that Matter</u>. Evans Books. Delta Systems.

A discussion book for the advanced student which covers controversial issues such as war, sex, women's position in society and euthenasia. The materials include extracts from books and newspapers, poems, photographs and cartoons. These provide several complimentary or opposing views on the subject and there are questions for discussion in class or for written work.

Grosset, Phillip. <u>What's Your Opinion</u>. Evans Books. Delta Systems.

A collection of discussion material for advanced students, including not only extracts from well-known books and poems, but also some previously unpublished essays by students. The passages present different aspects of subjects such as growing up, earning a living, racial prejudice and smoking, and are followed by questions, topics for further exploration and discussion and suggestions for written work.

Harkness, Shiona and John Eastwood. <u>Cue for a Drill</u>. Oxford University Press.

This book contains about 60 visuals including maps, time tables, charts, etc. with suggested grammatical drills.

Harmin, Merrill. <u>Got To Be Me</u>! Argus Communications.

This is a personal identity and self-awareness program for younger elementary students (but adaptable to other levels). It is based on 48 illustrated cards (96 sides) containing an unfinished sentence such as "I feel happiest when . . . " or "I wish I could . . ."

Harris, Jimmy G. and R. Hube. <u>On Speaking Terms: Conversational English for Advanced Students</u>. Collier MacMillan.

This book features 102 short dialogs on a variety of familiar subjects such as work, home, travel, leisure, health, people, and commuting. Every lesson centers around a short dialog of no more than ten lines. The conversations always take place between two unidentified people so that the students can feel natural playing the speakers' roles and can even inject a little of their own personalities into the dialogs. Many common figurative expressions are used.

Heaton, J.B. <u>Practice Through Pictures</u>. Longman, Inc.

There are 32 lessons in this book, each with a dialogue and with 12 pictures to use as substitution items in three different suggested question/answer exchanges.

113

Hill, L.A. Techniques of Discussion. Evans Books. Delta Systems.

It offers a wide range of frank, controversial discussion material on topics such as the influence of the mass media, the voting age for adolescents and violence in society. Each topic consists of a dialogue putting forward both sides of the argument, a passage expanding on them, exercises on selecting the key points of the argument and questions for further discussion. The topics are graded in difficulty of language and vocabulary and the book is written within a vocabulary of 3275 headwords.

Hill, L.A. and P.R. Polkin. Crossword Puzzle Books. Oxford University Press.

Puzzle books provide an informal way for students of English to check their command of the language. In each book there are three types of clues: pictures, simple definitions and sentences to be completed. The books are carefully graded according to the vocabulary they contain.

Hines, Mary Elizabeth. Skits in English. Regents Publishing Co.

There are 30 skits—10 are new, and the others revised so that the language and situations are completely contemporary. All are followed by questions and suggestions for role-playing activities that lead to improvisation.

Howe, Leland and M.M. Howe. Personalizing Education: Values Clarification and Beyond. Hart Publishers.

This handbook suggests a new way of relating to students. It helps teachers integrate values clarification strategies with the total curriculum. It extends the valuing process to other aspects of the classroom, for instance, organization and management.

Institute of Modern Languages (IML). Ideabook a resource manual for teachers of ESL for the Novice and the Pro. Institute of Modern Languages.

A practical resource book which serves as an introduction to various classroom strategies and activities. The book is loaded with puzzles, games, and easy-to-use suggestions to build communication skills. Hints and practical strategies on testing, error correction, methodology, and use of audio-visual materials make this book a very practical one for the language teacher's personal library.

Johnson, Jerilou. Living Language: Dialogs on Life in the United States. Newbury House Publishers.

This is a volume of practice dialogues and exercises for ESL/EFL students at the upper intermediate to advanced level. In ten conversational units, pupils learn syntax, vocabulary, and the nuances of American opinions and emotions regarding unemployment, family unity, divorce, single living, shopping, education, urban development, racism, and sexism. Students are prepared for the wide range of reactions they can expect from people in the United States.

Johnson, Kenneth G. et al, Nothing Never Happens. Glencoe Press.

A detailed syllabus for a general communication skills course, containing over 30 different classroom activities designed to help students get acquainted, develop an awareness of dysfunctional communication patterns, give experience in building group interaction and leadership skills. Excellent.

Lee, W.R. Language Teaching Games and Contests. Oxford University Press.

Designed to make language learning enjoyable, it includes suggestions suitable for use with all age groups and pairs, with outdoor as well as indoor games. Each chapter begins with a short introduction which describes the games it covers. In order to provide a quick and easy reference for the teacher each game is preceded by a diagram stating the language and age levels, the group size, and the use of the game. There is also a detailed structures index.

Maculaitis, Jean D'Arcy and M. Scheraga What to do Before the Books Arrive. Alemany Press, Ltd.

Classroom activities and lessons that the teacher can present without relying on a core text. An idea book that gives special attention to classroom management and values.

Markstein, Linda R. And D. Grunbaum. Sequential Picture Series. Longman, Inc.

This helps students develop speaking skills through creative exploitation of picture stories. Men, women, and children are protrayed in situations recognizable to all of us, such as an argument between friends, a moral dilemma, a new baby, a social faux pas and the loss of one's job. The stories encourage a gread deal of interpretation from the learners and engage their imagination. Students must use their powers of imagination and interpretation, and contribute their own knowledge, experience and feelings.

McCallum, George P. 101 <u>Word Games</u>. Oxford University Press.

This collection of word games can be a useful resource book in aiding the development and reinforcement of vocabulary building, spelling, conversation, and oral and listening practice. Each game is preceded by a list of required equipment, if any, and includes a summary of the appropriate vocabulary, sample answers, optimum group size, and level of difficulty. Notes to the teacher feature pointers for the successful presentation of games in the ESL classroom, as well as a discussion of possible pitfalls. A Structure Key is also provided.

McCallum, George P. <u>Seven Plays From American Literature</u>. English Language Service.

A volume of seven plays for intermediate and advanced students. They were chosen for their portrayal of American life and values, as well as for their dramatic interest. Each play is accompanied by a brief biographical sketch of the author, suggestions for production, and supplementary exercises. The plays were designed to be acted out in class. Each takes about fifteen minutes to perform.

McCallum, George P. <u>Six Stories for Acting</u>. English Language Service.

The materials in this book were chosen for their characterizations, suspense, and humor, and have been adapted to be read aloud or to be performed before and audience. After each play there are questions and exercises which can be used as a basis for discussions.

Methold, Kenneth. <u>English Conversation Practice</u>. Longman, Inc.

This book focuses on the important and difficult gap between "controlled" and "free" conversation. It incorporates guidance on what to say in typical situations, on appropriate intonation and gesture and shows the student how to turn the English of the classroom into the English of real life. It can be used as soon as the basic structures and lexis of English have been learned.

Molinsky, Steven J. And B. Bliss. <u>Side by Side: English Gramar Through Conversation</u>. Prentice-Hall.

A two-book series. Book One has 30 lessons, each focusing on a specific grammatical point. Introduced through conversation.

Moskowitz, Gertrude. <u>Caring and Sharing in the Foreign Language</u> Class. Newbury House Publishers.

This book is designed to help language teachers become aware of the insights which humanistic educational theory provides and learn how to apply such insights in order to foster real communication in the classroom. It emphasizes that teachers need to make educational experience relate to students' by helping students develop positive self-concepts.

Nelson, Gayle and T. Winters. ESL Operations. <u>Techniques for Learning While Doing</u>. Newbury House Publishers.

ESL operations provides ideas for role-playing situations. In addition, it uses high frequency action verb forms. There are follow-up exercises which are helpful when working on American intonation and stress patterns, vocabulary building, cultural information, word order, possessive pronouns, locative phrases, or adverbs. It contains Classroom Activities, Household Activities, Games and Exercises, Food and Recipes, Communication, Key Every Index and Grammar Notes Index.

Ockenden, Michael and T. Jones. <u>Around Town. Situational Conversation Practice</u>. Longman, Inc.

It presents informal conversational language. Forty-four situations are given, each in the form of four short dialogs, providing opportunities for pair practice, role-playing, group or individual work and self-study. It is illustrated with art and photographs.

Osman, Alice H. and J. McConochie. <u>If You Feel Like Singing</u>. Longman, Inc.

A collection of America's best-loved folksongs. Each of the 28 songs is prefaced by a reading on the origin and cultural significance of the song, a glossary of words and expressions not usually found in the dictionary. The words and music to the song follow, with guitar chords and notations.

Palmer, Adrian S. And M.C. Kimball. <u>Getting Along in English</u>. Longman, Inc.

This book consists of communication activities that integrate the practice of two important conversation skills: comprehending and conversing. In each of the twelve units, two types of oral communication activities and a vocabulary and writing exercise lead the student from "pseudo communication" to "autonomous communication." Dialog activities prepare the student for participation in the Discussion. In the Discussion student pairs converse fully on the subjects drawing from their own experience.

Phinney, Maxine Guin, et al. English Conversation Practices. University of Michigan Press.

Exercises in this text help students express their own thoughts in English by stimulating free conversation and giving students challenges. There are varied exercises which match the student's interests and abilities. Each lesson is organized around a central theme and provides opportunities for creative roleplaying.

Pifer, George W. and N.W. Mutoh. Points of View. Newbury House Publishers.

Presented here are 15 reading and discussion case studies for ESL students. There are two types of case studies. The Analysis section gives students practice in reading carefully and analytically. The second type of case study, Problem Solving, emphasizes group discussion. Both methods encourage students to develop and express personal points of view.

Price, Roger. Droodles. A price/stern/sloan humor classic.

This small booklet is a collection of Droodles which can be used and adapted for the ESL classroom. A Droodle is a drawing which doesn't make any sense until you know the correct title.

Regents Publishing Co. Picture It. Sequences for Conversation. Regents Publishing Co.

This text gives students an opportunity to practice English by describing sequences of pictures. The sequences depicted are essential, everyday situations, such as making a telephone call or buying clothes. It contains 480 ikllustrations with a question and answer for each picture, plus exercises for further practice. The book is intended for intermediate students and can accompany any basic text or program

Rooks, George. The Non-Stop Discussion Workbook. Newbury House Publishers.

This book presents problems for intermediate and advanced students of English. There are 30 discussion topics, ranging from life to death situations to planning a town, that are certain to involve students and promote discussion.

Simon, Sidney B., L. Howe and H. Kirschenbaum. Values Clarification. A handbook of practical strategies for teachers and students. Hart Publishers.

This book is designed to engage students and teachers in the examination of values. It contains 79 strategy situations, comlete with procedures and teacher's guide. Students are involved in practical experiences to make them examine their own feelings, ideas and beliefs, to relate values to their own decisions.

Stanford, Gene and A. Roark. Human Interaction in Education. Allyn and Bacon Publishing Co.

It offers an excellent cross-section of theory and method on the interactive part of education. Emphasis on practical applications: Group Development in the classroom, learning through group discussion, personal dimensions in discussions, role play, and simulations.

Taylor, Grant. English Conversation Practice. McGraw Hill.

This book contains nearly 300 pages of conversation divided into two parts—situational and structural. An index facilitates finding a topic or grammatical point.

Troyka, Lynn Quitman and Jerrold Nudelman. Taking Action: Writing, Reading, Speaking, and Listening Through Simulation-Games. Prentice-Hall.

This book gives students a chance to become involved in lifelike, adult experiences that are both challenging and fun. Each simulation-game encourages communicatin development by requiring students to read the simulation-game material, speak and listen within each game, and—as a direct, integrated follow-up—write in response to the demands of each situation. Following each simulation-game an extensive selection of "Communication Actions" provides additional experience in skill development. A resource chapter on communication skills is also included.

Winn-Bell Olsen, Judy E. Communication-Starters and Other Activities for the ESL Classroom. Alemany Press Ltd.

This book includes activities with tape recorders, cuisiniere rods, pictures, role plays, interviews, relays, bingo and other games adapted for ESL, activities for spelling, reading and writing in beginning classes, holiday activities and "special touches." Annotated Bibliography also included.

Pennant Education Materials. Film Strips and Cassettes for discussion materials.

Faces of Man is a filmstrip/cassette which explores the differences we encounter in the people we meet. It offers numerous possibilities for expression and individual themes. 78 frames, 6 minutes.

Feelings and Thoughts: How do you make decisions emphasizes that we must learn how to respond creatively to life's challenges. It examines the many aspects of human actions that go into making choices and delineates some of the methods we use. 80 frames, 8 minutes.

Friendly and Hostile: Understanding Inner Space demonstrates how our friendliness and hostility creates a mood wherever we are. 80 frames, 8 minutes.

Other People, Places and Things demonstrates the range of lifestyles, places, and cultures which represent the different ways people everywhere live their daily lives.

Perception: Do you see what I see? encourges the viewer to slow down and look at his or her world in depth and not fleeting glances. It urges a sharpening of awareness. 85 frames, 9 minutes.

Roles and Goals: Which Comes First, the Role or the Goal? concentrates on presenting diverse ideas which help young people formulate their own answers and guidelines. 77 frames, 6 minutes.

Pennant Educational Materials. Simulation Games.

Simulation are standouts, not only because they get students involved—mind and heart—in practicing basic communication skills but also because they require so little teacher-preparation time before they can be played. The teacher is freed to observe the action and give helpful feedback during the well-structured debriefings.

Dilema. This short simulation challenges players to consider which of six victims of a virus accident should receive a life-saving serum. The debriefing discussion concentrates on the ethics of group decision making, the effects of different leadership styles, and the ways that prejudice can distort the decision-making process. Time: 1–2 hours. Teacher Prep Time: 15 minutes.

Can of Squirms. Encourages meaningful, interesting dialogue between individuals. It can be used as a teaching tool or played as a fun game. Every can includes game elements, a leader's guide and 100 discussion questions. 11 different versions are available.

Match Wits helps players develop and understanding of the needs and the many values expressed in typical situations. The game emphasizes team play, one to five players per team, with participation by each of the team members. Game includes leader's guide with discussion questions, 64 situation cards, score cards, and instructions.

Join teaches students how to work together. In a small group, students work silently on solving a puzzle. The parts for eight squares are distributed randomly among the individual players, who must figure out how to coordinate their actions to solve the problem. Includes puzzle parts, instructions, Observer's Guide, and Debriefing Card.

Lifestyle Auction: Players bid competitively to try to "buy various lifestyle scenarios. The game expands the participants' view of the opportunites that are open to them. They gain new insights into their own values and are more informed about possible decisions in their own futures.

Sex Role Options: Pro's & Con's. This simulation deals with dramatic issues in the area of equal rights for women. To help participants become more aware of the complexity of the issues and their implications, Role Card instructions direct players to take particular stances, sometimes becoming "Devil's Advocates." Players: 7–16. Time: 45–90 minutes. Teacher Prep Time: 15 minutes!

Person to Person: Tuning In To Others. This game assists students in communicating more effectively. They take turns confiding problems and goals, and then responding helpfully to the other person. Response skills that are practiced include paraphrasing, showing interest, conveying empathy, observing body language, noting tone of voice, and challenging assumptions. Pages are color-coded to highlight the contrasting roles. Time: 30–60 minutes. Easelbook for each learner pair.